DANIEL ORR
REAL FOOD

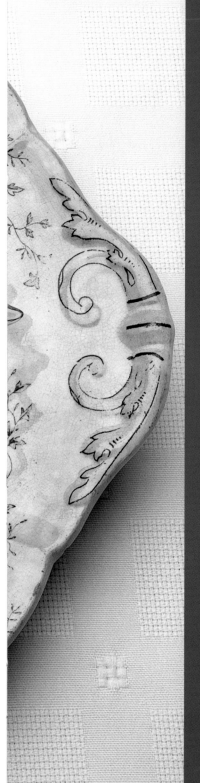

DANIEL ORR
REAL FOOD

SMART & SIMPLE MEALS AND
MENUS FOR ENTERTAINING

PHOTOGRAPHS BY SUSAN BROWN
DRAWINGS BY DANIEL ORR

RIZZOLI
NEW YORK

CONTENTS

seemingly sumptuous. There are no calorie counts or fat grams listed because this is not a diet, it is a way of life. Food should be thought-provoking, enjoyable, and memorable, not a source of anxiety.

The central theme of Regime Cuisine is an easy system of flavoring foods that makes them satisfying as well as lean and healthful. Spice blends from every corner of the world find their way into your oatmeal in the morning and your nighttime snacks—and the meals in between. Regime Cuisine also uses citrus juices and zest as well as a large variety of fresh herbs to replace or limit the use of salt and fat. Salt is, in most cases, a "to taste" ingredient in the recipes. For when you do use salt, I suggest a coarse-grained variety of sea salt that will add maximum flavor and a crunchy texture to your dishes.

Regime Cuisine is for every day. Breakfasts are quick and light, but give the comfort of the traditional American meal with influences from places like Brazil and Japan for health and added taste. Lunches, with the exception of a couple of warm sandwiches, are designed to be made ahead and eaten cold or at room temperature. Asian, Mediterranean, and Spanish cuisines make the dishes interesting and reinforce their significance in the development of the new American nutrition pyramid.

Regime Cuisine dinners are as varied, with recipes for every craving. These meals are easy to prepare, but they do challenge you to try different cooking techniques and new ingredients. The dinners are designed to be served as reasonable servings, with second helpings for the still-hungry. In fact you may find that the servings look larger than you are used to, but that you can eat more without feeling heavy. Leftovers make perfect lunches because they are so low in fat and may be eaten at room temperature or lightly reheated. Many are stream-lined versions of classic dishes that are homey and comforting.

Regime Cuisine soups are an example of that approach, and I have given them special attention. Many traditional soups start off as healthful combinations of vegetables, starches, and low-fat stocks.

They become less healthful, but oh so good, in the finishing. Veloutés, creamed soups, and bisques become dreamy with the heavy cream added at the end. The trick with Regime Soups is to make them as enjoyable as their richer cousins. Careful seasoning heightens their flavor and vegetable and starch purées—rather than flour and butter—give them body. Most Regime Soups may be eaten hot or chilled, and they freeze very well.

Snacks, desserts, and beverages haven't been forgotten; they are satisfying, fun, and intriguing.

To get started, review the equipment and the few pantry items you will find vital; once on hand, keep them within easy access to simplify

your daily cooking. Also included is a shopping list, which you can copy and use to check off the items you need on a weekly basis, then the few perishable items you need can be picked up from day to day.

Once Regime Cuisine has become ingrained into your lifestyle, it will be simply cooking. Then, the benefits of energy, lightness, clarity, and motivation will be so apparent there will be no turning back.

MENUS FOR ENTERTAINING

Entertaining is my business. As a professional chef I have cooked for such celebrated people as Prince Edward, Henry Kissinger, Diana Ross, and Madonna. But some of the most joyous times I have spent in the kitchen have been cooking at home for family, friends and my neighbor, Rose.

In the restaurant, I knock elbows with fifteen to twenty other guys in the kitchen. We are caught up in a quest for perfection for the folks on the other side of the wall. Each night after service, I mentally review the evening's highs and lows and design a strategy in the never-ending battle for excellence which begins early the next morning.

This is not what entertaining at home is or should be. It is about nurturing the gang you have called together, a time to give to others—not just recipes, but tales and jokes, a good ear, knowledge and understanding, and of course a stage for your guests to do the same.

Above all, entertaining well is not about being a slave in your kitchen looking out at your guests enjoying themselves. Although this is easier said than done, it is not impossible. Once you have learned the basic concepts and practiced the basic techniques by cooking Regime Cuisine day in and day out and you expand your planning skills, entertaining becomes not only easy, but a joy.

I most often entertain casually and I use the recipes from the Regime Cuisine section of the book because that way of eating helps me feel lighter and fresher. But special occasions, a visit from a friend from far away, or a good bottle of wine call for a different style of food—food that takes you to a different emotional level, touches the taste buds in a special way.

Regime Cuisine nourishes your body and allows you to feel good about what you eat on a daily basis. Meals for Entertaining satisfies those deep and very human needs that are beyond nutrition. These meals enlighten and bring happiness to those lucky enough to be sitting around your table.

EQUIPMENT FOR REGIME CUISINE

Blender or hand blender
Juicer
Nonstick pans
Spice grinder
Steamer

THE REGIME CUISINE PANTRY

In the Cupboard

Aloe extract
Arborio rice
Assorted dried and canned beans
Assorted seaweed
Balsamic vinegar
Barley
Basmati rice
Brown rice pasta
Buckwheat noodles
Canned octopus
Capers
Cellophane noodles
Chickpeas, dried and canned
Chili-corn pasta
Couscous
Dried figs
Honey
Instant polenta
Kosher salt
Lentils
Maple syrup
Miso paste
Oatmeal
Pine nuts
Raisins
Rice crackers

Rice flour bow-tie pasta
Sea salt
Sesame oil
Sesame seeds
Shredded coconut
Soy sauce
Spelt flour
Tamari paste
Unsweetened cranberry juice
Verbena tea
Walnuts
Wheat berries
Wild rice

Spices

Chilies
Cinnamon
Crushed red pepper (cayenne)
Curry powder
Master Blend (page 167)
Mellow Yellow (page 167)
Pickle masala
Russian Red Spices (page 167)
Saffron
Sweet Spices (page 167)

Fresh, Refrigerated, and Frozen Ingredients

Apples
Assorted herbs
Bean sprouts
Beets
Burdock
Butternut squash
Cabbage
Carrots
Celery
Cilantro
Coconut sorbet
Cucumbers

Eggplant
Eggs
Endive
Figs
Fresh berries
Fresh horseradish
Garlic
Ginger
Grapefruit
Haricots verts
Leeks
Lemons
Low-fat feta
Low-fat frozen yogurt
Melons
New potatoes
Nonfat yogurt
Onions
Orange juice
Oranges
Organic corn
Organic peas
Parsley
Parsnips
Pea shoots
Pears
Pita bread
Pumpernickel bread
Red onions
Scallions
Soy or almond cheese (page 32)
Spelt bagels
Spelt bread
Spinach
Tofu—firm and silken
Tomatoes
Turnips
Yellow squash
Zucchini

Overleaf, clockwise from top left: Irish Oatmeal Porridge with Pine Nuts and Raisins; Frozen Apple Cider with Winesap Apples; Poached Fillet of Beef "Pot-au-Feu" with Miso and Fresh Horseradish; Warm Vanilla "Cream" and Empress Rice Pudding; Shrimp on Rosemary Skewers with Barley Salad; Tandoori Salmon with Cabbage and Mashed Sweets.

DANIEL ORR

REGIME CUISINE

BREAKFASTS

4 egg whites

1 tablespoon honey

1 cup soy milk (see Note, page 18)

Pinch Master Blend (page 167)

1 tablespoon olive oil

¼ teaspoon orange-flower water or
    vanilla extract

½ teaspoon orange zest brunoise (page
    102)

6 slices sourdough, seven-grain bread,
    ¼ to ½ inch thick

Vegetable oil spray

Minted Yogurt (recipe follows)

Warm Berry Compote (recipe follows)

½ pint raspberries

Mint sprigs for garnish

SERVES 2

1 cup plain fat-free yogurt

¼ teaspoon lemon zest brunoise (page
    102)

10 to 15 mint leaves, cut into
    chiffonade

Pinch salt

MAKES 1 SCANT CUP

FRENCH TOAST WITH BERRY COMPOTE AND YOGURT

I usually serve this dish on weekends, when I can take the time to enjoy it. It is easy to double or triple the recipe for brunch entertaining. I make the Minted Yogurt and Warm Berry Compote the day before, so all I have to think about in the morning is the coffee.

In a large bowl whisk together the egg whites, honey, soy milk, Master Blend, olive oil, orange-flower water, and orange zest.

Submerge 3 slices of bread in the egg mixture until well soaked.

Place a 12-inch nonstick pan over medium-low heat. Remove the pan from the heat and spray it lightly with vegetable oil. Return the pan to the heat, put the soaked bread in the pan, and cook until golden brown. Turn and cook until the other side is brown, the toast is no longer spongy, and the egg mixture has firmed.

Place the French toast on a warm plate and repeat with the remaining slices.

Serve with dollops of Minted Yogurt and Warm Berry Compote and garnish with raspberries and mint sprigs.

MINTED YOGURT

This nicely accompanies breakfasts of fruit salad, pancakes, or cereal. It also adds zip to sandwiches and Middle Eastern or curried dishes.

Mix the ingredients thoroughly, then place in a very fine strainer or a colander lined with cheesecloth. Allow to drain at least 20 minutes or place, covered, in the refrigerator overnight.

HINT: For a dairy-free breakfast use the Regime Sour Cream (page 99).

WARM BERRY COMPOTE

½ pint berries such as raspberries, blackberries, blueberries, strawberries, or a mixture

4 tablespoons honey

¼ teaspoon Sweet Spices (page 167)

1 to 2 tablespoons lemon juice, depending on the sweetness of the fruit

¼ teaspoon lemon zest brunoise (page 102)

MAKES 1 SCANT CUP

Compotes are good on waffles, pancakes, or French toast. Leftovers may be chilled and used in place of jelly or jam.

Wash the berries and drain them on paper towels.

Heat the honey in a small sauté pan until it begins to bubble.

Add the berries, spices, and lemon juice and zest. Toss together with a spoon and immediately pour into a small serving dish. The fruit should be bruised by the heat, but not fully cooked.

On the left, French Toast with Berry Compote and Yogurt; right, Spelt Pancakes (page 22).

HOMEMADE CEREAL WITH APPLE JUICE

1½ cups raw rolled oats

¼ cup pecan halves

¼ cup walnut pieces

⅓ cup shredded coconut

⅓ cup white sesame seeds

1 tablespoon black sesame seeds

⅓ cup wheat germ

⅓ cup shelled sunflower seeds

¼ cup light brown sugar

¼ heaping teaspoon salt

¼ cup diced dried apricots

¼ cup raisins

Apple juice or soy milk (see Note)

SERVES 2

Although there is a little sugar in this recipe, the cereal is nothing like the store-bought variety; use even less sugar, if you like. A sliced banana is a good addition.

In a large, nonstick sauté pan cook the rolled oats, pecans, and walnuts over medium heat, stirring constantly so they toast evenly and don't burn, until they begin to brown, about 5 minutes.

Add the coconut, sesame seeds, wheat germ, and sunflower seeds to the pan. Lower the heat to medium-low and continue to toast, stirring, for 8 minutes more.

Sprinkle the brown sugar and salt evenly over the cereal and cook, stirring, for 3 to 5 minutes until the sugar melts and lightly coats each morsel.

Pour the cereal onto a baking sheet to cool. When it has cooled, add the dried apricots and raisins. Serve with apple juice or soy milk.

NOTE: There are many soy and rice milks on the market. Once available only in health food stores, they can now be found in high-end supermarkets. Most are sold in packaging, which allows them to be stored at room temperature, then chilled and used as needed. Most brands carry an assortment of flavors such as vanilla and carob as well as "original," which is closest to a dairy product.

HINTS: Other nuts, seeds, and dried fruit can be used in the mix. Always make small batches so your cereal stays fresh and crunchy and store it in an airtight container.

IRISH OATMEAL PORRIDGE WITH PINE NUTS AND RAISINS

1 cup whole Irish or Scotch oats

1 teaspoon salt

½ teaspoon orange zest brunoise (page 102)

½ cup raisins

2 tablespoons pine nuts

2 tablespoons pure maple syrup

Soy or rice milk (see Note, page 18; optional)

SERVES 2

There is nothing like oatmeal to keep you going when you have a big morning planned. I love to start a cold winter day with it, but find myself eating it year round. (Pictured on page 14.)

In a heavy-bottomed pan bring 2 cups water to a boil and add the oats and salt. Cook, stirring, until the mixture thickens slightly. Reduce the heat and simmer for 30 minutes, stirring occasionally. During the last 10 minutes of cooking, add the orange zest and raisins.

Lightly toast the pine nuts in a nonstick pan over medium heat.

Spoon the porridge into bowls and top each serving with pine nuts and syrup. Accompany with soy or rice milk if desired.

HINTS: Be careful not to overcook the oats, or you will lose the grain's texture and rich, nutty flavor. If you are using quick oats, follow the directions on the box.

Diced dried apples or apricots and walnuts can replace the raisins and pine nuts.

½ teaspoon grated fresh ginger

1 small clove garlic, minced

3 tablespoons low-sodium soy sauce

1 cup diced butternut squash

1 pound extra-firm tofu (page 28),
   diced

½ cup soaked kelpor wakame seaweed,
   roughly chopped (see Note)

2½ teaspoons miso paste, dissolved in
   ¼ cup water

½ teaspoon sesame oil

10 drops hot pepper sauce such as
   Tabasco

2 scallions, thinly sliced on a bias

¼ sweet red pepper, very finely
   julienned

¼ cup chopped cilantro

½ teaspoon white sesame seeds

½ teaspoon black sesame seeds

Juice of ½ lemon

Thin lemon slices cut into eighths

Salt

Freshly ground pepper

SERVES 2

POWER MISO SOUP

To Westerners it may seem strange to start the day with soup, but Asians have been breaking the fast with high-energy, low-fat eye-openers like this one for centuries. This spicy soup gives you a great lift any time.

In a medium-sized pot bring 2½ cups water to a boil and add the ginger, garlic, soy sauce, and squash. Return to a boil, then reduce the heat to a simmer and cook until the squash is tender but not cooked through.

Add the remaining ingredients, seasoning to taste with salt and pepper, and return the soup to a boil. Cook until it is just heated through and serve very hot in coffee mugs or soup bowls.

NOTE: Kelpor wakame seaweed can be found in most health food stores and Japanese markets.

BRAZILIAN FRUIT SALAD WITH HONEY AND SPICES

4 tablespoons honey

Juice of 1 lemon

Juice of 1 lime

½ teaspoon Sweet Spices (page 167)

1 mango, cut into cubes, squeeze the
   seed and reserve the juice

2 peaches, stoned and thinly sliced

1 papaya, skinned and seeded, cut into
   cubes

2 plums, stoned and thinly sliced

1 nectarine, stoned and diced

1 apple, peeled, cored, and diced

SERVES 4

The Brazilians I know have an innate skill for choosing the ripest, sweetest fruits at the market. Follow their example and when selecting fruit use your nose and sense of touch, and taste small fruit like cherries and berries. Often, farmers' market vendors will cut fruits and vegetables for you to sample. Fruit eaten by itself in the morning is cleansing.

In a large bowl mix together the honey, lemon and lime juices, and Sweet Spices. Add the fruit and toss gently. Chill thoroughly and toss again just before serving.

HINT: Add pomegranate seeds, berries, and other seasonal fruit when they are at the peak of flavor and omit those that are not. A few of the papaya seeds can be left in for their peppery flavor. If you like, add a banana, but only just before the fruit salad is served, or it will discolor and soften.

Spelt Pancakes

1 cup spelt flour

¼ teaspoon Sweet Spices (page 167)

¼ teaspoon baking powder

Pinch salt

2 to 3 turns of a mill with white pepper

¼ cup organic apple juice

¼ cup soy milk (see Note, page 18)

1 tablespoon safflower oil, plus a little
    for brushing the pan

2 egg whites

3 tablespoons honey

½ cup blueberries, washed

1 cup diced apples, mangoes, or pears

Juice of ½ lemon

Mint sprigs for garnish

Regime Sour Cream (page 99) or
    nonfat yogurt

SERVES 2

Lead belly syndrome often sets in after most Sunday morning pancakes—you feel more like going back to bed than making the most of your day. Spelt flour, which is available in health food stores, has far less gluten and is easier to digest than regular flour, so these pancakes won't slow you down. Fruit in pancakes makes them seem lighter, and the blueberries give a sweet, acid punch. (Pictured on page 17.)

In a medium-sized mixing bowl mix the flour, Sweet Spices, baking powder, salt, and white pepper.

In another bowl combine the apple juice, soy milk, oil, egg whites, and 1 tablespoon of the honey and whisk together until the honey dissolves.

Pour the wet ingredients into the dry, and add the blueberries. Gently fold the ingredients together with a rubber spatula; do not stir and overwork the batter.

Brush a 12-inch nonstick pan with safflower oil and place over medium heat. Spoon the batter into the pan to make 4 large pancakes; cook until bubbles form on the surface of the pancakes and the bottoms are nicely browned. Turn the pancakes and cook the other side. Place 2 pancakes on each serving plate and keep them in a warm place.

In the same pan over medium-high heat, combine the remaining honey and the diced fruit. Cook until the honey begins to caramelize, then add the lemon juice. Spoon the fruit over the pancakes, garnish with the mint sprigs, and serve with the Regime Sour Cream.

NOTE: Diced bananas make a great variation.

TOASTED SPELT BAGELS WITH TOFU CREAM CHEESE AND REFRIGERATOR JAM

Warm breads, pastries, and coffee are the cornerstones of a Continental breakfast, but most breakfast pastries harbor hidden fats, not to mention what we put on them. Spelt or seven-grain—even traditional—bagels are fat free and lower in calories than pastry. The protein-packed Tofu Cream Cheese (page 99) and honey-sweetened Refrigerator Jam (page 99) add enough moisture to the bagels, so that butter or dairy cream cheese won't even be missed. Serve one toasted bagel per portion, and offer about ¼ cup of walnut halves along with the "cream cheese" and jam. Spelt bagels are available in the frozen food section of most health food stores.

Egg White Omelet Soufflé with Warm Tomato Salsa

FOR THE SALSA

1 tablespoon olive oil

3 cloves garlic, minced

1 medium onion, finely diced

1 jalapeño pepper, seeds and
   membrane removed, minced

¼ teaspoon chili powder

Pinch cumin seeds

1 teaspoon tomato paste

2 beefsteak tomatoes or 4 plum
   tomatoes, diced

3 scallions, thinly sliced on a bias

3 tablespoons chopped Italian parsley

3 tablespoons chopped cilantro

Salt and freshly ground pepper

FOR THE OMELET

6 egg whites

½ teaspoon ground turmeric

¼ teaspoon salt

5 turns of a pepper mill

2 teaspoons olive oil

1 ounce grated soy cheese (see Note,
   page 32)

1 bunch watercress

1 teaspoon olive oil

Juice of ½ lemon

Salt and freshly ground pepper

SERVES 2

Mild yellow turmeric adds color to the whipped egg whites in this recipe, so you won't miss the fatty yolks. Make sure you have everything prepared in advance so you can serve this breakfast hot from the oven. It's great with toasted spelt bread or seven-grain bread.

To make the salsa, heat the oil in a small, nonreactive saucepan over medium heat, then add the garlic, onion, jalapeño, chili powder, cumin, and tomato paste. Cook for 5 to 8 minutes, stirring often so that the vegetables do not stick to the pan.

Add the tomatoes, scallions, parsley, and cilantro, and season to taste with salt and pepper. Remove from the heat and keep in a warm place until ready to serve.

Preheat the oven to 450° F.

Whip together the egg whites, turmeric, salt, and pepper until the mixture forms soft peaks.

Heat a 6-inch nonstick sauté pan over medium-high heat. Add 1 teaspoon of the oil and swirl the pan so that it is evenly coated with the oil on the bottom and sides.

Pour half the egg white mixture into the pan and sprinkle with half the soy cheese. Place in the oven and bake until the egg whites are just set in the center, 5 to 7 minutes, then carefully remove the omelet to a warm plate. Repeat with the remaining egg white mixture and soy cheese for the second omelet.

Meanwhile, wash the watercress and dry it well. Top the omelets with several spoonsful of the salsa and a few sprigs of watercress. Toss the remaining watercress in a bowl with 1 teaspoon oil and the lemon juice. Season to taste with salt and pepper. Serve the omelets with the extra salsa and the watercress salad in serving bowls on the table.

HINTS: I have two small nonstick pans so I can prepare both omelets at the same time. This also allows me to serve four at brunch without too much waiting.

Chilled leftover salsa is great on baked potatoes with Regime Sour Cream (page 99) and a drizzle of olive oil.

LUNCHES

2 (5- to 6-ounce) pieces center cut
  salmon fillet

Salt and freshly ground pepper

2 very thin lemon slices

1 teaspoon white vinegar

½ pound soba noodles, fresh if possible

1 tablespoon tahini

2 tablespoons low-sodium soy sauce

½ tablespoon white sesame seeds

½ tablespoon black sesame seeds

½ teaspoon chopped fresh ginger

½ clove garlic, chopped

Juice of ½ lemon or more if needed

½ teaspoon lemon zest brunoise (page
  102)

1 tablespoon brown rice vinegar

1 teaspoon toasted sesame oil

¼ cup chopped walnuts

3 scallions, thinly sliced on a bias

5 turns of a pepper mill

Pinch crushed red pepper

1 large head red or white endive or a
  mixture, washed

Italian parsley or cilantro sprigs for
  garnish

1 sweet red pepper, julienned
  (optional)

SERVES 2

COOL BUCKWHEAT NOODLES WITH STEAMED SALMON

Spicy sesame noodles have long been a staple on Chinese menus. I've lightened the recipe and added intrigue with the lemon zest and endive. (Pictured on page 29.)

Season the salmon with salt and pepper and place a thin slice of lemon on each piece.

Put ¼ inch of water in a small pan, cover, and bring to a boil. Add a pinch of salt and the white vinegar.

Place the salmon in the pan, return the water to a boil, then reduce the heat and cover. Steam the salmon for 4 to 6 minutes, depending on its thickness, until just cooked through. Remove the salmon from the water, leaving the lemon slice on the fish. Cover the fish with moist paper towel and let it cool to room temperature, then chill it in the refrigerator.

Bring a large pot of salted water to a boil, add the noodles, and cook until they are al dente. Drain, rinse, and chill under cold water, then set aside in the refrigerator.

Combine the tahini, soy sauce, sesame seeds, ginger, garlic, lemon juice and zest, rice vinegar, sesame oil, walnuts, scallions, pepper, and crushed red pepper to make a dressing. Mix well and adjust the seasoning with salt, pepper, and lemon juice.

Toss the pasta with the dressing and let it sit for 10 to 15 minutes before serving. To serve, place the endive leaves around the edge of a platter. Put the pasta in the center and top with the salmon. Garnish with the parsley and red pepper.

HINTS: The salmon is also nice served warm over the cool, spicy pasta as a contrast. Poached chicken, shrimp, scallops, or steamed mussels can be substituted for the salmon. Add hot pepper sauce to the dressing if you like more heat. Chopped cilantro or mint can also be added.

Five-Grain Salad with Raisins, Bean Sprouts, and Crushed Hazelnuts

½ cup medium barley, cooked, rinsed, and chilled

½ cup wheat berries, cooked, rinsed, and chilled

½ cup French or green lentils, cooked and chilled

½ cup wild rice, cooked and chilled

½ cucumber, peeled, seeded, and diced

½ cup corn kernels, blanched and chilled, or thawed frozen corn

½ cup crushed hazelnuts

½ cup raisins

1 cup mung bean sprouts or other large sprouted beans

3 tablespoons olive oil

Juice of 1 lemon

1 teaspoon lemon zest brunoise (page 102)

Juice of 1 lime

1 clove garlic, minced

1 small red onion, thinly sliced

½ teaspoon Mixed Pepper Blend (page 167)

½ teaspoon salt

10 turns of a pepper mill

½ cup roughly chopped Italian parsley

SERVES 2

Although this recipe makes a large quantity, it won't last long. I love a big bowl of it after a workout. It can be quite elegant when served with a salmon fillet that has been dusted with curry and a sprinkle of sea salt and steamed and chilled. Try other grains for new textures and tastes. See the instructions for cooking grains on page 170.

In a large bowl combine the barley, wheat berries, lentils, rice, cucumber, corn, hazelnuts, raisins, and bean sprouts.

In another bowl, whisk together the olive oil, lemon juice and zest, lime juice, garlic, onion, Mixed Pepper Blend, salt, and pepper.

Toss the dressing with the grains and adjust the seasoning; sprinkle with the parsley and serve.

HINT: Grains such as barley, wheat berries, wild rice, and even some beans and lentils can be cooked, rinsed, chilled, packed in small freezer bags, and frozen. They defrost quickly and allow for streamlined preparation of dishes such as this one and Risotto of Five-Grains (page 58).

Pages 28–29, clockwise from top left: Spicy Harvest Vegetables; Flaked Tuna with Creste di Galli Pasta and Curry Vinaigrette; Cool Buckwheat Noodles with Steamed Salmon; Tangled Greens with Herbs, Croutons, and Feta; Couscous Salad with Octopus and Seaweed; Oven Grilled "Cheese" Sandwich; Herbed Turkey Burger; Tofu with Haricots Verts and Corn Salad. Center: Poached Seafood with Glass Noodles.

ON TOFU

Tofu, so plain, so bland, also is one of the most versatile of all foods. Daybreak can bring tofu to the table as "cream cheese" (page 99) to spread on bagels. Midday it may be served marinated and chilled or as a whipped miracle in place of mayonnaise for any sandwich. At dinner, tofu may show up as rouille for bouillabaisse (page 41), as curried steaks, or as meaty chunks in my Big Miso Dinner Soup (page 60). Factor in the nutritional benefits of tofu—high protein, low fat, low calories—and you make the case for tofu as a basic food that should always be on hand.

When I shop for tofu, I choose among the many varieties available. I use fresh locally made cakes from Chinatown or other Asian shops for cooked dishes, the kind that comes in sealed packages for chilled marinated dishes. Silken tofu usually completely fills its container, whereas firm tofu most often is surrounded by packing liquid. New packages of nonperishable tofu are beginning to appear outside the refrigerated cases. Although the packages are a little smaller, the quality is good for dips and sauces.

Most tofu is better when some of its liquid is removed. To do this, turn a plate over on a small tray to catch the liquid. Place the tofu on the upturned plate and weight it with a second plate; let the tofu sit for 15 to 20 minutes, then discard the liquid and continue with your recipe.

Here is an "at-a-glance" guide to the basic tofu types:

- *Silken:* sauces, vinaigrettes, dips, creams, and as melt-in-your-mouth cubes in soups

- *Firm:* "cream cheese" and thicker dips and spreads

- *Extra firm:* dishes in which tofu is the center of attention, where its texture allows it to stand proud

ROASTED STRIPED BASS WITH ONIONS AND POTATOES

1 pound wild striped bass fillet, skin on

1 teaspoon coarse sea salt

10 turns of a pepper mill

½ teaspoon Master Blend (page 167)

2 tablespoons olive oil

1 medium onion, sliced

4 cloves garlic, roughly chopped

1 sprig thyme

5 fingerling potatoes or 3 small Yukon Golds or white new potatoes, cut into ½-inch pieces

3 Red Bliss potatoes, cut into ¼-inch slices

1 sweet potato, peeled and diced

Juice of 1 lemon

Salt

Freshly ground pepper

SERVES 2

Rustic dishes look great when served in their cooking vessels. If you have a cast-iron pan or a nice copper one that you would like to take to the table, this is the time. You can start the fish and potatoes in a nonstick pan on the stovetop, then heat your serving pan, spray it with a little vegetable oil, transfer the ingredients to it, and finish cooking the dish in the oven.

Preheat the oven to 450° F.

Sprinkle the fish with the sea salt, pepper, and Master Blend on both sides.

Heat a 10-inch nonstick pan over medium-high heat. Add 1 tablespoon of the oil, then place the bass in the pan, skin side down.

Reduce the heat to medium and cook until the skin becomes crisp, 5 to 7 minutes. With a spatula, remove the fish to a plate.

Add the remaining oil to the pan, then add the onion, garlic, thyme, and potatoes. Sauté over medium to medium-high heat until the potatoes are three-quarters cooked and the onions begin to caramelize, 8 to 10 minutes.

Place the fish on top of the potatoes, skin side up, and place the pan on the center rack of the oven. Roast for 8 to 10 minutes until the fish and the potatoes are cooked through and crisp on the outside. (The cooking time will vary with the thickness of the fish.)

Sprinkle with the lemon juice, season to taste with salt and pepper, and serve piping hot.

NOTE: You can use other firm, thick-fleshed fish such as tile, shark, swordfish, or cod. If you use cod, salt it first (see Peppered Cod, page 50).

HINT: I like to use the sprig of thyme roasted with the potatoes as a garnish; the thyme can be replaced with rosemary or sage.

PEPPERED COD FILLET WITH SHRIMP FRIED SAFFRON RICE

1 pound skinless, boneless center cut cod fillet, cut into 2 pieces, each 1½ inches thick

2 tablespoons coarse sea salt

1 tablespoon Mixed Pepper Blend (page 167)

1 tablespoon roughly chopped thyme leaves

1 tablespoon olive oil

1 medium onion, finely diced

3 cloves garlic, minced

2 pinches saffron threads

½ pound spinach, washed, squeezed dry, and finely chopped

1 tablespoon Chinese fermented black beans

½ jalapeño pepper, seeds and membrane removed, minced

2 cups cooked Scented Basmati Rice (page 97)

¼ pound small shrimp, shelled

Salt

Freshly ground pepper

Cilantro sprigs

SERVES 2

There is a Cuban-Chinese restaurant in my neighborhood that looks like it has been there for 20 years. It was the inspiration for this dish of stir-fried Cuban yellow rice and fermented black beans with peppered cod. Salting the fish first firms it and keeps it from falling apart.

Place the cod in a bowl and sprinkle with the sea salt. Let sit for 15 to 20 minutes, then rinse under cold water and pat dry.

Combine the Mixed Pepper Blend and the thyme and spread the mixture over the cod.

Heat a 12-inch nonstick pan over high heat, add the oil, and carefully place the cod in the pan. Cook the cod until nicely browned on one side, then turn and cook until the second side is browned and the cod is cooked through, 7 to 10 minutes. If the cod is not cooked through but is browned, lower the heat and continue to cook for 2 to 3 minutes, taking care not to overcook the fish. Remove the cod to a warmed plate and cover to keep warm.

Place the onion, garlic, and saffron in the pan and cook over medium heat until the onions are soft but not browned. Add ½ cup water and bring to a boil. Add the spinach and cook until it is just wilted. Add the shrimp, fermented black beans, jalapeño, and rice and heat through. Season to taste with salt and pepper. (Remember, the black beans are salted, so taste before adding extra salt.)

Place the rice in a warmed serving dish, top with the cod, and garnish with cilantro.

NOTE: Bass, salmon, tilefish, or snapper may be used in place of cod. If you use another fish, it is not necessary to salt the fish as described in the recipe; simply add a bit of sea salt with the Mixed Pepper Blend and thyme.

FOR THE SALMON

½ clove garlic, minced

½ teaspoon minced fresh ginger

1 teaspoon lemon zest brunoise (page 102)

Juice of ½ lemon

¼ teaspoon pickle masala or a few drops hot pepper sauce

¼ teaspoon Mellow Yellow (page 167) or curry powder

1 teaspoon ground turmeric

10 turns of a pepper mill

2 tablespoons Regime Sour Cream (page 99) or fat-free yogurt

2 (6-ounce) pieces salmon fillet, 1 to 1¼ inches thick

FOR THE SWEET POTATOES

2 medium sweet potatoes, peeled and roughly cut into 1-inch cubes

1 tablespoon olive oil

1 teaspoon honey

Salt

Freshly ground pepper

FOR THE CABBAGE

1 tablespoon olive oil

1 medium onion, julienned

2 cloves garlic, minced

2 cups shredded Napa cabbage

¼ teaspoon caraway

Salt

Freshly ground pepper

Opal basil, basil, or Italian parsley

SERVES 2

TANDOORI SALMON WITH CABBAGE AND MASHED SWEETS

A *tandoor* is a traditional Indian oven used for baking breads and roasting meats. Usually the meats are skewered, then marinated in a yogurt and spice sauce colored with red dye. The dye is used in India, but it is now thought that the original color was more of a saffron yellow, and many finer Indian restaurants here have stopped using the dye. (Pictured on page 14.)

For the salmon, mix together the garlic, ginger, lemon zest and juice, pickle masala, Mellow Yellow, turmeric, and pepper. Fold in the Regime Sour Cream. Spread the marinade over the salmon and refrigerate for 45 minutes.

Meanwhile, steam the sweet potatoes until they are soft, then mash them with the oil, honey, and salt and pepper to taste. Cover to keep warm.

For the cabbage, heat the oil in a nonstick pan over medium-high heat, add the onion and garlic, and sauté until they are soft but not browned. Stir in the cabbage and caraway and cover. Cook for 3 to 4 minutes, until the cabbage is tender; if the cabbage begins to brown, add 2 to 3 tablespoons water. Season to taste with salt and pepper.

Preheat the broiler. Place the salmon with its marinade in a nonstick pan with a metal handle and place it under the broiler near the heat for 5 to 10 minutes, depending on the thickness of the salmon. The marinade should brown and become crusty on top, and the salmon should be moist in the center; do not overcook.

Place the cabbage mixture on a small serving platter and arrange the salmon fillets over; garnish with the herbs. Serve the sweet potatoes in a warm bowl on the side.

HINT: If the salmon fillet is thin, place it very near the heating element of the broiler and cook it quickly.

SAUTÉED BAY SCALLOPS AND NEW POTATOES WITH MESCLUN

6 small potatoes such as new red or white potatoes, creamers, or fingerlings

Salt

½ pound mesclun salad with bitter greens

¾ pound bay scallops, largest available

3 turns of a pepper mill

1 teaspoon Master Blend (page 167)

1 tablespoon olive oil

4 cloves garlic, sliced into rounds

½ teaspoon fresh thyme leaves

¾ teaspoon coarse sea salt

4 tablespoons balsamic vinegar

Juice of 1 lime

10 sprigs dill

SERVES 2

This is a one-dish meal that will feed two hungry people or four as a first course. I like this salad because the sweetness of the scallops and potatoes is highlighted by the acidity of the vinegar and lime. It is important to use the crystals of sea salt—their crunch makes the dish sparkle.

Cover the potatoes with water in a medium-sized saucepan and add a pinch of salt. Bring to a boil, then reduce the heat to a simmer. Cook for 15 to 20 minutes until the potatoes slip from a dinner fork when pierced. Refresh under cold water until they are cool enough to handle, cut them into quarters, and set aside.

Wash and dry the mesclun salad. Place half at the centers of 2 plates, leaving room around the edges; set aside in a cool place.

Toss the scallops with the pepper and Master Blend.

Heat a 10- or 12-inch nonstick pan over high heat. Add the oil, then the potatoes, and cook for 10 to 15 minutes. Turn the potatoes once and allow them to brown slightly, then add the garlic. Cook until the garlic is just colored; do not let the garlic burn or it will become bitter.

Keep the heat high and add the scallops to the pan. Cook them without moving them until they are caramelized on one side, about 3 minutes.

Add the thyme and sea salt and toss the mixture lightly to distribute the seasonings. Remove from the heat. Deglaze the pan with 2 tablespoons of the vinegar and immediately spoon the potatoes and scallops over the salad. Add the remaining 2 tablespoons of vinegar and the lime juice to the pan, scraping any browned bits with a spatula, and stir to make a sauce. Spoon the sauce around the salad and garnish with the dill.

NOTE: Choose bay scallops that are large, plump, and dry—not surrounded by a lot of milky liquid.

HINTS: Try not to move the scallops much while cooking them or they will lose their juices. Top-quality scallops need very little cooking. If they are nicely browned on one side, they are cooked. Do not be concerned if the scallops release a lot of their juices; let the liquid reduce completely, and the scallops will then caramelize.

It is best to use the potatoes immediately, but they can be cooked up to 24 hours in advance if necessary and reheated.

COUSCOUS WITH CURRIED SHRIMP AND SQUID

1 cup couscous

2 tablespoons olive oil

1 clove garlic, minced

1 small carrot, peeled and julienned

1 rib celery, julienned

½ white onion, julienned

1 medium turnip or celery root, peeled and julienned

½ leek, washed well and julienned

½ zucchini, julienned

½ yellow squash, julienned

½ sweet red pepper, julienned

2 teaspoons Mellow Yellow (page 167) or curry powder

½ pound squid, cleaned and cut into rings

½ pound medium shrimp, peeled, deveined, and butterflied

¼ cup Regime Sour Cream (page 99)

1 small apple, peeled, cored, and diced

½ cup roughly chopped cilantro

4 to 8 drops hot pepper sauce

Salt

Freshly ground pepper

Cilantro sprigs for garnish

Juice of 1 lime

SERVES 2

M any modified low-fat recipes aren't as appealing as the original because they lose richness. But here, tofu sour cream makes all the difference. The recipe can be varied with colorful seasonal vegetables.

Cook the couscous following the instructions on the box and keep covered.

Heat the oil in a 12-inch nonstick pan over high heat. Add the garlic and the vegetables. Stir in 2 to 3 tablespoons water and 1 teaspoon of the Mellow Yellow and cook, stirring often, until the water evaporates. With a spoon, remove the vegetables to a bowl.

In the same pan over high heat cook the squid and shrimp with the remaining Mellow Yellow just until they are opaque, about 2 minutes.

Return the vegetables to the pan and add the Regime Sour Cream, apple, and chopped cilantro. Mix well and season to taste with the hot pepper sauce, salt, and pepper. Pour onto a platter, garnish with cilantro sprigs, sprinkle with lime juice, and serve with the couscous in a separate bowl.

HINTS: Spicy food needs to be balanced in a meal with less aggressive, starchy dishes. Many cuisines, such as Mexican, Chinese, and Indian, use rice for this purpose, but in Morocco couscous fills the bill. You can cook it in advance and reheat it in the microwave oven for about 3 minutes. Try whole-wheat couscous for a more tabbouleh-like texture.

I use a mandoline to cut the carrots, celery, turnip, zucchini, and yellow squash. In any case, cut the vegetables as thin as possible, so they will not need much cooking.

Try this recipe with tofu in place of seafood. Use extra-firm tofu that has been pressed for 15 to 20 minutes between two plates to remove excess liquid; cut it into ½-inch cubes. Sliced chicken can also be used.

STEAMERS WITH BROWN RICE FUSILLI

½ pound brown rice fusilli

2 tablespoons olive oil

1 shallot, minced

2 cloves garlic, sliced into thin rounds

½ cup dry white wine

2 bay leaves

¼ teaspoon crushed red pepper

4 large cremini mushrooms

1 ½ pounds steamer clams (or cockles, mussels, or littlenecks), scrubbed

1 pint small cherry or pear tomatoes

20 basil leaves, cut into chiffonade

½ teaspoon lemon zest brunoise (page 102)

Juice of ½ lemon

Salt

Freshly ground pepper

SERVES 2

This is a quick and simple dish I make following an afternoon workout. Sometimes I replace the pasta with kale greens, mustard greens, or Swiss chard and serve it with a side dish of brown rice.

Bring a large saucepan of water to a boil. Add the pasta and cook until it is just al dente; drain the pasta, refresh it under cold water, and drain well.

In the same pan over medium-high heat place the oil, shallot, and garlic. Cook until the garlic just begins to color, then add the wine, bay leaves, crushed red pepper, mushrooms, clams, and half the tomatoes. Toss well in the liquid and cook until the clams open, 5 to 7 minutes. Remove the clams to a bowl. If using steamers, carefully remove the black glove that covers the neck of the clam and gently rinse away any sand.

To the saucepan, add the pasta, the remaining tomatoes, the basil, lemon zest, and lemon juice and stir to incorporate. Return the clams to the pan, raise the heat to high, and season to taste with salt and pepper. Serve immediately on a heated platter.

HINT: I like to add more crushed red pepper or some minced jalapeño pepper to spice this dish up a bit.

BIG MISO DINNER SOUP

4 cups Vegetable Stock (page 166) or water

1 tablespoon minced fresh ginger

1 clove garlic, chopped

½ acorn squash, seeds removed, washed under hot water, peeled if necessary, and cut into bite-size pieces

2 ears fresh or frozen corn, shucked, silk removed, quartered

1 medium onion, peeled and cut into eighths

2 carrots, peeled and cut into 2-inch pieces

½ head Savoy cabbage, cut into ½-inch wedges

8 large mushrooms

½ pound spinach, washed, tough stems removed

1 pound firm tofu (page 28), cut into 1-inch squares

2 scallions, cut into 1-inch pieces

2 tablespoons red miso

1 tablespoon tamari or soy sauce

5 drops hot pepper sauce such as Tabasco

Juice of ½ lemon

¼ teaspoon sesame oil

Salt

Freshly ground pepper

SERVES 2

This is a "hands-on" meal. I love to feel connected to what's on my plate, but so many so-called spa meals are too delicately presented. Get out your biggest soup bowls, roll up your sleeves, and forget your table manners. This is a meal to share with your closest friends. Don't forget to put an empty bowl in the middle of the table to discard your cleaned corncobs.

In a large pot bring the stock to a boil and add the ginger and garlic.

Add the squash, corn, onion, carrots, cabbage, and mushrooms and return to a boil. Cook at a low boil until the cabbage and onions are three-quarters cooked, 5 to 7 minutes.

Add the spinach, tofu, and scallions and return the soup to a boil. Cook until the tofu is heated through and the spinach is wilted, 2 to 3 minutes.

Using a slotted spoon, transfer all the vegetables to a large, warmed serving bowl, cover the bowl and keep it in a warm place.

Add the miso, tamari, hot pepper sauce, lemon juice, and sesame oil to the broth. Season to taste with salt and pepper.

Pour the broth over the vegetables and serve at once.

HINT: Scallops, shrimp, or diced chicken breast can be added during the last 5 minutes of cooking.

CURRY BRAISED TOFU WITH BASMATI RICE, LENTILS, DRIED CHERRIES, AND PICKLE MASALA

1 cup French Le Puy lentils or other
green lentils

2½ cups Vegetable Stock (page 166)
or water

1 bay leaf

1 sprig fresh thyme

¾ teaspoon salt

3 turns of a pepper mill

1 recipe Scented Basmati Rice (page 97)

1 tablespoon olive oil

2 medium onions, thinly sliced

2 cloves garlic, chopped

1 teaspoon minced fresh ginger

1 tablespoon tomato paste

1 teaspoon curry powder

¼ teaspoon pickle masala

Juice of 1 orange

1 teaspoon orange zest brunoise (page 102)

¼ cup dried cherries

1 large tomato, roughly chopped

¼ cup basil, cut into chiffonade

1 pound firm tofu (page 28)

Salt

Freshly ground pepper

Basil sprigs

SERVES 2

This is my favorite type of dish, one that incorporates flavors from all over the world. Here French lentils, Middle Eastern spices and rice, Asian ginger and tofu, and American dried cherries are creatively combined.

Put the lentils in a pot, cover them with 1½ cups stock, and bring to a boil. Skim the surface and add the bay leaf and thyme; simmer for 15 to 20 minutes, until tender, adding more liquid if necessary. Add the salt and pepper in the last 5 minutes of cooking; drain and set aside.

Heat a large saucepan over medium-high heat. Add the olive oil, then the onions, garlic, ginger, tomato paste, curry powder, and pickle masala. Cook, stirring, for 5 minutes, then add 1 cup stock, orange juice and zest, and dried cherries. Bring to a boil, then lower the heat and simmer for 5 minutes more. Add the tomato and basil and cook to heat through.

Heat the tofu in the sauce or in a steamer or microwave oven (covered with plastic wrap). Spoon the curried vegetables over the tofu.

Serve the rice, lentils, and tofu in separate bowls and garnish with the basil.

NOTE: The basil may be replaced with a mixture of half mint and half parsley.

GRILLED PORK TENDERLOIN WITH CIDER VINEGAR, APPLE-ROSEMARY ORZO, AND KALE

1 to 1¼ pounds trimmed pork tenderloin (2 small or 1 large tenderloin)

½ tablespoon Sweet Spices (page 167)

1 tablespoon Mixed Pepper Blend (page 167)

3 tablespoons cider vinegar

1 teaspoon coarse sea salt

¾ cup orzo pasta

2 tablespoons olive oil

1 medium onion, diced

1 clove garlic, minced

1 Granny Smith apple, cored and diced

1 teaspoon chopped rosemary

½ teaspoon lemon zest brunoise (page 102)

Juice of ½ lemon

½ cup roughly chopped Italian parsley

Salt

Freshly ground pepper

2 cloves garlic, thinly sliced

⅓ pound kale, tough stems removed, cut into chiffonade

Rosemary sprigs for garnish

SERVES 2

Pork tenderloin is one of the leaner meats around. Grilling pork is always successful: the meat seems to be made to pick up the smoky flavors. Cider vinegar, apples, and rosemary complete the orchestra that will play a symphony in your mouth.

Rub the pork with the Sweet Spices, Mixed Pepper Blend, 2 tablespoons of the vinegar, and the sea salt. Allow to marinate for 10 to 15 minutes.

Prepare a charcoal fire.

Cook the orzo in boiling water until it is just al dente, drain, rinse in cold water, and drain well.

Place a medium-sized nonstick pan over medium-high heat, add 1 tablespoon oil, the onion, and minced garlic and sauté until the onion is soft. Add the apple, rosemary, lemon zest and juice, parsley, salt and pepper to taste, and the orzo and heat through. Pour into a dish, cover, and set aside in a warm place.

In the same pan over high heat place ½ tablespoon oil and the sliced garlic. Cook until it smells toasty and just begins to color. Quickly add the kale and toss to coat it with the garlic and oil. Pour in ½ cup water and steam the kale, uncovered, until it wilts and the water has completely evaporated. Season to taste with salt and pepper.

Grill the pork for 8 to 15 minutes, depending on the heat of the coals, the size of the tenderloins, and the distance the meat is from the heat. The pork should be slightly pink in the middle.

Remove the pork to a small plate, cover with foil, and allow the meat to rest for 5 to 10 minutes. Reserve the juices that run out of the meat.

To serve, place the orzo and kale on a serving platter. Slice the pork and arrange it on the platter. In a small bowl combine the remaining vinegar and ½ tablespoon oil with the meat juice and spoon it over the meat. Garnish with rosemary sprigs and serve.

HINTS: Do not overcook the pork: because of the lack of fat marbling in the meat, it will become quite dry. Try this dish with veal tenderloin.

You can also sear the meat on all sides in a nonstick pan over high heat with 1 tablespoon olive oil, then roast in a hot oven, turning several times.

CAULIFLOWER SOUP WITH LOW-FAT SPICED CROUTONS

½ head cauliflower

½ russet potato

1 medium Spanish onion

2 cloves garlic, peeled

4 shallots, peeled

½ cup 1-percent milk

5½ cups Chicken Stock (page 166)

½ teaspoon ground cumin

12 turns of a mill with white pepper

1½ teaspoons salt

Juice of ½ lemon

2 hard-boiled egg whites, chopped

¼ cup chopped parsley

Low-Fat Spiced Croutons (recipe follows)

4 sprigs dill or cilantro

MAKES 2 QUARTS

SERVES 4

Roughly chop the cauliflower, potato, onion, garlic, and shallots and place them in a saucepan. Add the milk, stock, cumin, white pepper, and salt. Bring to a boil, then reduce the heat to a simmer and cook until the vegetables are very soft. Purée the soup in a blender or with a hand mixer, then pass it through a fine sieve, pressing the solids with a ladle to extract the liquid. Season to taste with lemon juice, salt, and white pepper.

Mix the eggs and parsley together.

To serve, ladle the soup into warm bowls. Spoon a bit of the egg mixture into the center of each bowl and top with the croutons. Garnish with dill sprigs. (Pictured opposite.)

LOW-FAT SPICED CROUTONS

4 slices firm white bread

½ teaspoon curry powder

½ teaspoon ground cumin

¼ teaspoon ground turmeric

1½ teaspoons extra-virgin olive oil

Freshly ground white pepper

Preheat the oven to 450° F. Remove the bread crusts and cut the bread into small cubes. Place the bread on a baking sheet and bake, stirring often, until the cubes are browned on all sides. In a medium-sized mixing bowl combine the spices and oil. Toss the croutons in the mixture and season to taste with white pepper.

Clockwise from bottom left: Mushroom Velouté; Chilled English Pea Soup with Mint; Regime Pistou; Cauliflower Soup with Low-Fat Spiced Croutons; Spring Onion Soup with Saffron and Spices; Tomato Soup Perfumed with Fennel.

BUTTERNUT BISQUE

1 medium butternut squash, peeled, seeded, and roughly chopped

½ tablespoon olive oil

1 medium onion, roughly chopped

3 cloves garlic, peeled and roughly chopped

¾ teaspoon salt

½ teaspoon Mellow Yellow (page 167)

⅛ teaspoon freshly ground white pepper

Zest of ½ lemon, cut into brunoise (page 102)

MAKES 1 ½ QUARTS

SERVES 4

Place the squash and 3¼ cups water in a large stock pot and bring to a boil.

Meanwhile, heat a medium to large sauté pan over medium-high heat. Put the oil, onion, garlic, salt, Mellow Yellow, white pepper, and lemon zest in the pan and cook gently, stirring often, until the onion is soft, 7 to 8 minutes. If the onion begins to color, add a spoonful of water from the pot to the pan.

Add the onion mixture to the pot with the squash; continue to simmer until the squash is very soft. With a slotted spoon, remove the squash, onion, garlic, and a little of the cooking liquid to the bowl of a food processor or blender, and purée.

Return the purée to the pot of cooking liquid and stir to incorporate. Taste and adjust the seasoning with salt, white pepper, and Mellow Yellow. Serve hot. (Pictured on page 69.)

HINT: For a more refined velouté, pass the soup through a fine strainer.

SPRING ONION SOUP WITH SAFFRON AND SPICES

2 tablespoons olive oil

3 cloves garlic, minced

4 cups thinly sliced spring onions (see Note), 8 to 10 large onions, or 3 large Spanish onions

½ teaspoon lemon zest brunoise (page 102)

¼ teaspoon saffron threads

¼ teaspoon Master Blend (page 167)

2 fresh bay leaves

2 branches thyme

1 cup white wine

3 to 4 cups Vegetable or Chicken Stock (page 166)

Salt

Freshly ground pepper

SERVES 6 TO 8

I came up with this soup when I saw the beautiful onions in the market. Saffron immediately came to my mind. What could be sunnier and more uplifting? What could be more different from the comforting red wine and beef stock in the rich classic French onion soup that soothes the soul in winter? (Pictured on page 69.)

In a large saucepan over medium heat, heat the oil and add the garlic; sauté until the garlic is slightly browned, then add the onions, lemon zest, saffron, and Master Blend. Mix well, then add ¼ cup water and simmer until the onions are tender, 30 to 45 minutes.

Add the bay leaves, thyme, and wine and bring to a boil; cook for 5 minutes. Add the stock, bring to a simmer, and cook for 20 minutes longer. Season to taste with salt and pepper.

NOTE: Spring onions are those sweet first onions of the year that still have their green tops attached. They vary in size. The ones I call for are on the large side. If you like, thinly slice some of the tops for garnish. The rest can be used in Asian- or Mexican-style dishes in place of scallions, or in stocks.

HINT: This soup also makes a striking sauce for roasted or grilled fish. Serve the fish on a bed of sautéed spinach and surround it with the bright yellow sauce.

SNACKS

PUMPERNICKEL CROSTINI WITH YELLOW TOMATO CONCASSÉ AND MARINATED SOY

FOR THE PUMPERNICKEL CROSTINI

5 slices pumpernickel bread

1 tablespoon olive oil

5 turns of a pepper mill

2 pinches salt

1 clove garlic, minced

FOR THE YELLOW TOMATO CONCASSÉ

4 large yellow tomatoes

10 basil leaves, cut into chiffonade

1 anchovy fillet, minced

1 small clove garlic, minced

1 tablespoon olive oil

Salt

Freshly ground pepper

FOR THE MARINATED SOY

½ cup firm tofu (page 28) or soy cheese
  (page 32), cut into ¼-inch dice

1 clove garlic, smashed to a paste

Juice of ½ lemon

1 teaspoon olive oil

5 basil leaves, cut into chiffonade

Freshly ground pepper

Sea salt

Basil, purple or green sprigs

SERVES 4

Preheat the oven to 250° F.

To make the crostini, cut the bread into quarters. Place the bread on a baking sheet and bake until they are crisp, 45 minutes to 1 hour. Turn the oven off, leaving the bread inside.

In a large bowl combine the oil, pepper, salt, and garlic and mix well. Add the crisp bread slices and toss them in the garlic mixture to lightly coat. Place the slices back on the baking sheet and return them to the cooling oven for 15 minutes, then let the crostini cool to room temperature.

Peel, seed and dice the tomatoes, then toss them together with the remaining ingredients for the Tomato Concassé. Season to taste with salt and pepper.

Combine the ingredients for the Marinated Soy in a small bowl, seasoning to taste with salt and pepper.

Top the crostini with Tomato Concassé, then Marinated Soy. Garnish with basil sprigs and a few grains of sea salt. (Pictured on page 77.)

POPCORN WITH HOMEMADE HERB SALT

¼ cup popcorn, popped in a steam or microwave popper

1 teaspoon extra-virgin olive oil

Herb Salt (page 164)

MAKES 2 QUARTS

I'm one of those crazy people who takes his own popcorn to the movies. I won't pay those prices for junk food—I'll make it myself! However, it isn't junk food if it is steamed or popped in a fat-free microwave popper. It has a satisfying crunch and, when perfumed with herb or curry salt, more flavor than the artificial butter variety. (Pictured on page 77.)

Place the popcorn in a large bowl. Drizzle with olive oil, toss, and season to taste with Herb Salt.

BAKED PITA CRISPS

6 pieces pita bread

2 tablespoons olive oil

10 turns of a pepper mill

¼ teaspoon salt

1 large clove garlic, finely minced or smashed to a paste

SERVES 4

Preheat the oven to 250° F.

Cut the pitas into quarters, split each quarter into 2 pieces and place on a baking sheet. Bake until crisp, 45 minutes to 1 hour; turn the oven off, leaving the pitas inside.

In a large bowl combine the oil, pepper, salt, and garlic and mix well. Add the pitas and toss them in the garlic mixture to lightly coat them. Place the pitas back on the baking sheet and return them to the cooling oven for 15 minutes. Let the crisps cool to room temperature. Serve with Sunny Salsa (page 97) or Regime Eggplant Caviar (page 81) and store the leftovers in an airtight container. (Pictured on page 77.)

HINT: To make garlic paste, smash the garlic clove with the side of a chef's knife and finely mince it. Sprinkle the garlic with a pinch of salt, and use the side of the knife to crush and spread the garlic into a paste.

DIPS

Those dips are so good, you'll find yourself planning meals around them. They are great in vegetable pita pockets; curried tuna or chicken sandwiches; with poached fish, garlic, and herbs; with pasta salad; and in burritos or chilled tortilla wraps with hot peppers and cilantro.

CURRY DIP

1 cup Regime Sour Cream (page 99)

¼ pound extra-firm tofu (page 28), squeezed to remove excess water

1 small clove garlic, peeled

1 teaspoon chopped fresh ginger

1 teaspoon curry powder

½ teaspoon ground turmeric

Pinch pickle masala or 5 drops hot pepper sauce such as Tabasco

½ teaspoon sea salt

1 teaspoon lemon zest brunoise (page 102)

Juice of 1 lemon

MAKES APPROXIMATELY 2 CUPS

Combine all the ingredients in a food processor or blender and purée until very smooth. Pour into a storage container and chill at least 1 hour.

HINT: Don't be concerned if the dip looks a little thin when it is in the blender. It will set when chilled. If you want a thicker dip, add more extra-firm tofu.

SUN-DRIED TOMATO AND ROSEMARY DIP

15 sun-dried tomato halves

1 cup Regime Sour Cream (page 99)

1 clove garlic, peeled

1 tablespoon chopped fresh rosemary

Salt

5 turns of a pepper mill

2 tablespoons pine nuts, toasted in nonstick pan and roughly chopped

MAKE APPROXIMATELY 2 CUPS

Finely chop 8 of the sun-dried tomatoes and set them aside.

In a food processor or blender combine the remaining sun-dried tomatoes, the Regime Sour Cream, garlic, and rosemary and purée until the mixture is smooth.

Season with salt to taste and the pepper and fold in the chopped sun-dried tomatoes and pine nuts. Thin if too thick with water and adjust the seasoning as necessary.

NOTE: Choose soft sun-dried tomatoes with a vibrant color. The amount of salt will vary with the salt content of the sun-dried tomatoes.

Clockwise from top: Popcorn with Homemade Herb Salt; Un-Deviled Eggs (the filling is made with mashed potatoes, herbs, and turmeric); Garlic and Herb Dip; Endive Barquettes with Wild Rice and Apple Salad; Hot Pepper and Cilantro Dip; White Bean Purée with Japanese Rice Crackers; Pumpernickel Crostini. Center: Sunny Salsa and Baked Pita Crisps.

GARLIC AND HERB DIP

½ cup basil leaves

½ cup Italian parsley leaves

2 tablespoons rosemary leaves

1 cup Regime Sour Cream (page 99)

¼ pound extra-firm tofu (page 28),
    squeezed to remove excess water

1 clove garlic, peeled

2 tablespoons chopped chives

2 tablespoons fresh thyme leaves

1 tablespoon chiffonaded mint leaves

Salt

Freshly ground pepper

½ teaspoon lemon zest brunoise (page
    102)

MAKES APPROXIMATELY 2 CUPS

Bring 2 cups water to a boil and blanch the basil, parsley, and rosemary for 1 minute. Drain, refresh under cold water, and squeeze to remove excess water. Combine the Regime Sour Cream, tofu, and garlic in a food processor or blender and purée until smooth. Add the blanched herbs and purée until the mixture is very smooth and uniformly green. Fold in the chives, thyme, and mint and season to taste with salt and pepper and the lemon zest. (Pictured on page 77.)

HOT PEPPER AND CILANTRO DIP

1 cup Regime Sour Cream (page 99)

¼ pound firm tofu (page 28), squeezed
    to remove excess water

1 roasted pimento packed in vinegar

1 clove garlic, peeled

1 teaspoon cumin

½ teaspoon salt

5 turns of a pepper mill

1 tablespoon chopped pickled jalapeño
    pepper

¼ cup chopped cilantro

MAKES APPROXIMATELY 2 CUPS

In a food processor or blender combine the Regime Sour Cream, tofu, pimento, garlic, ½ teaspoon cumin, salt, and pepper and purée until the mixture is very smooth and the pimento has uniformly colored the dip. Fold in the remaining cumin, the jalapeño, and cilantro. Taste and adjust the seasoning as necessary. (Pictured on page 77.)

ENDIVE BARQUETTES WITH WILD RICE AND APPLE SALAD

1½ cups packed cooked wild rice

1 shallot, minced

1 apple, peeled, cored, and finely diced

1 tablespoon olive oil

Juice of ½ lemon

¼ teaspoon lemon zest brunoise (page 102)

1 teaspoon honey

¼ teaspoon curry powder

½ teaspoon Sweet Spices (page 167)

5 turns of a pepper mill

¼ teaspoon salt

10 mint leaves, finely chopped

2 to 3 heads Belgian endive

SERVES 4

These small endive boats make perfect fat-free canapés. I also fill them with different bean purées, grain salads, or fillings made with Tofu Cream Cheese (page 99). Serve them on a platter of mixed hors d'oeuvres for a healthful start to a dinner party. (Pictured on page 77.)

Toss together all the ingredients except the endive. This may be made up to 24 hours in advance. Taste and adjust the seasoning just before serving.

Separate the endive leaves from the core and fill them with the rice salad. Alternatively, place the salad in a bowl and arrange the endive leaves around the edge of the bowl. Let your guests use the endive to scoop up the rice salad.

WHITE BEAN PURÉE

2 tablespoons olive oil

1 medium onion, diced

1 teaspoon lemon zest brunoise (page 102)

2 cloves garlic, minced

2 (15-ounce) cans white beans, or 1 pound white beans cooked until very soft

1 teaspoon rosemary, chopped

Pickle masala or chili powder

Salt

Freshly ground pepper

1 tablespoon chopped Italian parsley

Rosemary sprigs for garnish

SERVES 2

This spread is great with one of the many varieties of Japanese rice crackers in health food stores these days—the ones with seaweed flakes are my favorite. It can also be spread on sandwiches and pita bread. For more formal party canapés you can use a piping bag to dispense the purée onto crackers. (Pictured on page 77.)

In a medium-sized saucepan combine 2 tablespoons water, 1 tablespoon of the oil, the onion, lemon zest, and garlic. Bring to a boil, then reduce the heat and cook until the water has evaporated and the onion is soft. Let cool to room temperature.

Drain the beans well and, reserving ¼ cup for garnish, place the rest in a food processor with the chopped rosemary, ¼ teaspoon pickle masala, ½ teaspoon salt, and the onion mixture. Purée until very smooth.

Season to taste with salt and pepper. Pour into a serving bowl and place in the refrigerator to chill.

Before serving, sprinkle the top with the remaining beans, the remaining olive oil, a small pinch of pickle masala, and the parsley. Garnish with rosemary sprigs.

HINT: If you like a little more zip, add a few drops of hot pepper sauce and the juice of ½ lemon.

REGIME EGGPLANT CAVIAR

4 cups diced eggplant, with peel
  (2 medium or 6 Japanese eggplants)

Juice of 1 lemon

2 cups diced onions

2 cloves garlic, minced

1 teaspoon salt

10 turns of a pepper mill

1 tablespoon olive oil

2 tablespoons red wine vinegar

1 teaspoon lemon zest brunoise
  (page 102)

½ teaspoon Mellow Yellow (page 167)

½ cup chopped Italian parsley

Salt

Freshly ground pepper

MAKES 2 ½ TO 3 CUPS

Traditional eggplant caviar is full of olive oil, but I've reduced the fat in this version, so feel free to spread plenty on sandwiches or pumpernickel crostini or use it as a dip for Baked Pita Crisps (page 75).

In a heavy-bottomed, nonreactive saucepan combine the eggplant, lemon juice, ½ cup water, onions, garlic, salt, and pepper. Bring to a boil, then reduce the heat and simmer, covered, until the eggplant and onions are very soft, 10 to 15 minutes. Uncover and continue to cook until the liquid evaporates, 15 to 20 minutes. The eggplant should look almost like a purée.

Pour into a medium-sized mixing bowl and let the mixture cool to room temperature.

Add the oil, vinegar, lemon zest, Mellow Yellow, parsley, and salt and pepper to taste and place in the refrigerator to chill. The Eggplant Caviar will keep for 3 to 5 days, covered, in the refrigerator, or longer if frozen.

DESSERTS

1 cup basmati rice

Salt

½ teaspoon cinnamon

1 teaspoon orange zest brunoise
(page 102)

1 cup mixed dried fruit such as white
and black raisins, currants, and
diced apricots

¼ teaspoon vanilla extract

½ cup honey

½ teaspoon grated fresh ginger

½ teaspoon Sweet Spices (page 167)

⅓ cup orange juice

2 (7-gram) packages powdered gelatin

10½ ounces firm silken tofu (page 28)

Raspberry-Orange Coulis (recipe
follows)

Mint sprigs for garnish

SERVES 6

EMPRESS RICE PUDDING WITH HONEY, CINNAMON, AND RASPBERRY-ORANGE COULIS

This updated version of the French dessert *riz à l'impératrice* is a staple of my regime kitchen. (Pictured on page 14.)

In a saucepan bring the rice and 2½ cups water to a boil. Add a pinch of salt, cover, and simmer until the rice is tender, about 20 minutes. Taste the rice to check for doneness. Add up to ½ cup more water if needed. Drain the rice and let it cool to room temperature.

In a mixing bowl combine the cinnamon, orange zest, dried fruit, vanilla, honey, ginger, and Sweet Spices; set aside.

Combine the orange juice and gelatin in a glass bowl and allow the gelatin to soften. Cover the dish with plastic wrap and cook in a microwave oven for about 1 minute until the gelatin is dissolved. Alternatively, melt it in a double boiler.

Purée the tofu in a blender until smooth, add the gelatin mixture, and continue to blend until thoroughly combined. Fold the tofu into the dried fruit mixture.

Fold in the rice and season to taste with a pinch of salt and more honey or Sweet Spices, if necessary.

Pour the mixture into a glass bowl and chill in the refrigerator until it is thoroughly set, 1½ to 2 hours or overnight.

Spoon onto dishes with a bit of Raspberry-Orange Coulis and garnish with mint sprigs.

RASPBERRY-ORANGE COULIS

1 cup raspberries

¼ cup honey

Juice of 1 lemon

¼ cup orange juice

MAKES 1 CUP

Gently rinse the raspberries and place them on a paper towel to dry.

In a small saucepan bring the honey, lemon juice, and orange juice to a boil. Remove the pan from the heat and immediately add the raspberries; stir to incorporate.

Purée the mixture in a blender or with a hand mixer until it is smooth. Pass the purée through a fine strainer to remove the seeds. Chill well. The coulis keeps for 3 to 5 days, covered, in the refrigerator, or 1 month if frozen.

FIGS WITH HONEY AND SPICES

¼ cup red wine such as Burgundy or Zinfandel

Juice of 1 orange

1 teaspoon orange zest brunoise (page 102)

1 teaspoon Sweet Spices (page 167)

3 tablespoons honey

1 pint (8 to 10 pieces) fresh Black Mission figs (see Note)

Juice of 1 lemon

3 mint leaves, cut into chiffonade

2 scoops nonfat vanilla frozen yogurt

2 sprigs mint for garnish

SERVES 2

In a 6-inch sauté pan bring the red wine, orange juice and zest, Sweet Spices, and honey to a boil, then reduce the heat to a simmer.

Remove the tough tops of the fig stems and, using a sharp knife, cut a double X about ⅓ of the way down through the tops.

Add the figs to the wine mixture and cook over medium heat until they are tender and the liquid has reduced and thickened slightly, 10 to 12 minutes; do not overcook the figs. If the figs are tender but the liquid has not reduced, remove the figs and continue to cook the syrup until it is thick.

Using a slotted spoon, transfer the figs to individual serving plates, placing the figs in a circle with a small space in the center.

Cook the syrup until it is reduced to a glaze, add the lemon juice and chiffonaded mint, and spoon the glaze over the figs. Place a small scoop of frozen yogurt in the middle of each plate and garnish with the mint sprigs.

NOTE: If figs are out of season, use moist, high-quality dried figs and simmer them in water until they soften. Dried figs have a richness that cries out winter as strongly as fresh figs scream summer.

VERBENA POACHED PEARS WITH BLACKBERRIES

1 cup honey

1 fresh vanilla bean, cut in half lengthwise, or 1 teaspoon vanilla extract

2 bunches fresh lemon verbena

3 peppercorns, coarsely crushed

4 thin lemon slices

4 firm Bosc or Anjou pears

½ pint blackberries

Lemon verbena or mint sprigs for garnish

SERVES 4

Poached pears chilled in a little of their juice with blackberries, as in this recipe—or with a granité—are a refreshing finale to a summer meal. On cooler days, the pears can be caramelized in a nonstick pan with a little of the poaching liquid and served with vanilla frozen yogurt.

Place 3 cups water and the honey in a medium-sized saucepan and bring to a boil. Stir well to incorporate the honey, which will sink to the bottom.

Add the vanilla bean, verbena, pepper, and lemon and allow to steep, barely simmering, for 30 minutes.

Peel the pears. With a melon baller core the pears from the bottom, leaving the stems intact. Place them in the poaching liquid and return to a boil. Reduce the heat to a simmer and poach until the pears are tender, 25 to 35 minutes, depending on the type and size of the pears. (If you plan to reheat the pears, remove them while they are slightly firm.)

Allow the pears to cool to room temperature in the poaching liquid, then place in the refrigerator to chill.

To serve, place each pear in a small dish, surround with blackberries, and garnish with a sprig of verbena.

NOTE: Lemongrass, sage, or lemon thyme can be substituted for the verbena; however, use slightly less.

HINT: You can fill the bottoms of the pears with pear or blackberry sorbet just before serving. When serving the pears warm, try filling them with a mixture of chopped dried fruit, walnuts, and a sprinkle of brandy.

FROZEN GRAPES WITH GRAPPA

Seedless grapes, an assortment of white, red, and black, left on their stems

Very cold grappa (optional)

Some historians say that frozen grapes were the first sorbet, eaten right off the vines after an early frost. They must have been refreshing. I often eat them in bed when I get my late-night sweet toothaches. Chill the grappa in the freezer.

Rinse the grapes thoroughly and dry them. Place the grapes on a plate or in a bowl and freeze; when they are frozen, transfer them to a freezer bag.

To serve, snip off bunches of the grapes and place on plates with shots of grappa in chilled glasses.

HINT: I sometimes serve this as a palate cleanser during wine tastings. The grappa revives the appetite. (The French use Calvados brandy in place of grappa—they call it *Le Tru Normande*.)

MINTED MELON "SOUP" WITH RASPBERRIES

1 honeydew or cantaloupe melon

1 cup orange juice

Pinch salt

½ cup white wine such as Chablis

2 tablespoons honey (optional)

10 mint leaves, cut into chiffonade

½ pint raspberries, gently washed

Mint sprigs for garnish

SERVES 6

Cut off the ends of the melon to stabilize it on the cutting board, then remove the rind. Cut the melon in half and remove the seeds.

Cut half the melon into large chunks and place them in a blender with the orange juice, salt, and wine. Add the honey if the melon is less sweet than you prefer. Blend until smooth, pour the mixture into a bowl, and stir in the chiffonaded mint; chill thoroughly in the refrigerator.

Dice the remaining melon and add it to the soup. To serve, ladle the soup into chilled bowls and top with the raspberries and mint sprigs.

1 cup blueberries

1 pint fat-free vanilla frozen yogurt

⅛ teaspoon Sweet Spices (page 167)

¼ teaspoon lemon zest brunoise (page 102)

Juice of ½ lemon

Mint sprigs for garnish

Fresh strawberries and blueberries

FOR THE MINTED STRAWBERRIES

20 strawberries, washed, trimmed, and thinly sliced

8 mint leaves, cut into chiffonade

2 tablespoons honey

Juice of ½ lemon

SERVES 4

BLUEBERRY BOMBE WITH MINTED STRAWBERRIES

Timing is the most critical element in this preparation: have your bowls and mold thoroughly chilled, and work fast. The bombe is made the day before, and the dessert is assembled just before serving. The blueberries can be replaced with a little cocoa powder for a chocolatey, marbled effect.

Gently wash and dry the blueberries, spread them out on a platter or baking sheet, and place in the freezer until the berries are frozen.

Line a 1½-pint mold or bowl with plastic wrap and place it in the freezer to chill thoroughly.

Let the frozen yogurt soften slightly. In a chilled mixing bowl, beat the yogurt until it is smooth, but do not let it fully melt.

Quickly fold in the blueberries, Sweet Spices, lemon zest, and lemon juice and pour the mixture into the prepared mold. Place the mold in the freezer for 6 to 8 hours or until the bombe is firm.

For the minted strawberries, toss together the ingredients and set aside for at least 10 minutes.

To serve, unmold the bombe and cut it into 4 equal pieces. Place each piece on a chilled dessert plate with a few of the Minted Strawberries and their juice. Decorate with sprigs of mint and the remaining strawberries and blueberries.

ORANGE FILLETS WITH COCONUT SORBET AND TOASTED COCONUT

2 tablespoons shaved fresh coconut (see Note) or packaged unsweetened coconut

2 Navel oranges

8 mint leaves, cut into chiffonade

2 teaspoons honey

Pinch cinnamon

2 scoops dairy-free coconut sorbet

2 sprigs mint for garnish

SERVES 2

In a nonstick pan over medium-high heat toast the coconut until it is uniformly brown. Remove to a plate to cool.

With a sharp paring knife, peel the oranges, cutting just below the bitter white pith. Cut into segments, or "fillets," by cutting out the flesh from between the membranes. Squeeze the leftover membranes to extract the juice.

Add the chiffonaded mint, honey, and cinnamon to the orange segments and place in the refrigerator to chill thoroughly.

Arrange the segments in flower patterns in two chilled bowls. Pour half the juice into each bowl, top with the sorbet, and garnish with the coconut and mint sprigs.

NOTE: If you are using fresh coconut, use a vegetable peeler to shave the coconut into $1/4$- to $1/2$-inch slivers.

QUICK PEACH SORBET

1½ pounds frozen peeled peaches, left at room temperature for about 10 minutes

½ cup honey

1 cup muscatel wine

Blueberries and mint sprigs for garnish

SERVES 6

Muscatel dessert wine and honey are perfect matches for peaches, complementing but never overpowering their subtle flavors.

In a food processor combine the peaches, honey, and wine and blend until smooth. Place the mixture in plastic containers and place in the freezer for 30 to 45 minutes. Scoop the sorbet into chilled bowls and garnish with blueberries and mint.

Warm Vanilla "Cream"

2 vanilla beans

10½ ounces silken tofu (page 28)

½ teaspoon vanilla extract

About ¼ cup honey

2 egg whites

¼ teaspoon lemon zest brunoise
    (page 102)

½ teaspoon lemon juice

2 turns of a mill with white pepper

Pinch salt

SERVES 6

Richness is a state of mind. We all crave creamy desserts and we all punish ourselves for lack of will power, but sometimes we can have our cake and eat it too. Served with scoops of fat-free chocolate sorbet, this simple dessert allows just that: the combination of warm and cold teases the mouth into believing it is getting away with more than it is. (Pictured on page 14.)

Preheat the oven to 250° F.

Split the vanilla beans lengthwise and scrape out the seeds; save the pods for another use. Combine all the ingredients in a blender and purée until very smooth and light. Taste and adjust the seasoning with additional honey, if needed.

Let the mixture sit for 10 to 15 minutes, tapping the blender bowl occasionally to release air bubbles.

Pour the mixture into small ramekins, place the ramekins in a water bath, and place in the oven. Bake for 30 minutes and serve warm.

HINTS: You can make a fat-free "crème brûlée" by chilling the "custards," sprinkling them with raw sugar that has been reduced to dust in a coffee grinder, and browning the tops lightly under the broiler or with a blow torch. If using the broiler, place the ramekins as close to the heat as possible.

Vary the flavor by placing chopped semisweet chocolate, candied ginger, or praline paste in the bottoms of the ramekins before you pour in the "cream."

BEVERAGES

Squeezing, juicing, or blending your own fruit and vegetable drinks is a true expression of self love. You'll consider the cleanup time well worth it, once you experience the flavor of these homemade elixirs. It is true that many of the dietary fibers you get from whole fruits and vegetables are lost in juicing, but these juices are quick and refreshing alternatives to soft drinks—enjoy them in addition to whole fruits and vegetables.

Making juices at home allows you to control what goes into them. Many juice stands don't wash or peel the ingredients, and large companies add stabilizers or must pasteurize their juices before packaging and shipping. Juices are most nutritious when enjoyed straight from the press. Even within 15 minutes, oxidation begins to diminish its health value. For this reason, I chill the ingredients slightly before juicing to slow the process.

Choose firm fruits and crisp vegetables for juicing. A perfectly ripe pear or pineapple tastes so sweet, and the texture may melt in your mouth, but in a juicer it will melt too, producing more of a purée than a juice. If your beverage is too thick, simply thin it with a little orange juice.

Combining your "home brew" with orange juice, organic cider or apple juice, or sparkling water provides the maximum bang for your buck. I add these when I'm making juices for large groups of friends at brunches or cocktail parties. Apple ice cubes are great in any of the juice drinks.

So make room on the counter for your juicer or blender—probably the most challenging aspect of making juices.

Clockwise from top left: Deep Green Spinach, Parsley, and Celery Juice; Pineapple and Honeydew with Basil; Apple and Cranberry Elixir; Fresh Carrot, Ginger, and Passion Fruit Cocktail; Beet "Sangria" with Winesap Apples; Pear Juice with Lemon and Ginger.

FRESH CARROT, GINGER, AND PASSION FRUIT COCKTAIL

15 peeled organic carrots

1-inch piece ginger

1 cup passion fruit juice (see Note)

1 cup orange juice

MAKES 1 QUART

Press the carrots and ginger through the juicer, followed by the juices. (This will help to extract any of the remaining flavors from the vegetable pulp.)

NOTE: Bottled passion fruit juice may be found in Brazilian and Caribbean markets.

BEET "SANGRIA" WITH WINESAP APPLES

4 winesap apples, or other firm apple, cut into wedges

½ lemon with peel, cut into wedges

5 medium beets

Grapes, orange wedges, or apple slices for garnish

MAKES 1 QUART

Press the apples and lemon through the juicer, followed by the beets. Serve over ice, garnished with fresh fruit.

COOL CUCUMBER AND ALOE FRAPPÉ WITH LEMONGRASS

1 cucumber, diced

3 ribs celery

1 Granny Smith apple, diced

1 stalk lemongrass, cut into 4 pieces

½ lemon with peels, cut into wedges

¼ cup aloe juice (available in health food stores)

MAKES 1 QUART

Press the cucumber, celery, apple, lemongrass, and lemon through the juicer and stir in the aloe juice.

6 firm Bosc pears, quartered

½ lemon with peel, cut into wedges

1½-inch piece ginger

1 stalk lemongrass, cut into 4 pieces

¼ cup aloe juice (available in health
    food stores)

MAKES 1 QUART

8 firm apples such as Granny Smith or
    winesap, cut into pieces

½ lemon with peel, cut into wedges

2 tablespoons unsweetened cranberry
    concentrate (see Note)

6 apple juice ice cubes

MAKES 1 QUART

½ pineapple, peeled but not cored,
    cut into pieces

½ honeydew melon, rind and seeds
    removed, cut into pieces

8 basil leaves, 3 cut into chiffonade

1 cup orange juice

MAKES 1 QUART

PEAR JUICE WITH LEMON AND GINGER

Press the ingredients, in the order given, through the juicer.

HINT: You can also add a little white wine and serve the drink over ice cubes.

APPLE AND CRANBERRY ELIXIR

Press the apples and lemon through the juicer (the lemon prevents the apples from discoloring), stir in the cranberry concentrate, and serve over the ice cubes.

NOTE: Unsweetened cranberry concentrate can be found in health food stores.

PINEAPPLE AND HONEYDEW WITH BASIL

Press the pineapple, honeydew, and the whole basil leaves through the juicer. Stir in the orange juice and the chiffonaded basil leaves.

HINT: Very cold vodka can be added to this juice for special occasions.

Deep Green Spinach, Parsley, and Celery Juice

½ pound spinach

1 cup parsley leaves

2 ribs celery

2 green apples

¼ teaspoon celery salt

3 turns of a pepper mill

MAKES 1 QUART

Press the spinach, parsley, celery, and apples through the juicer. Stir in the celery salt and pepper.

Cabbage and Watercress Cleansing Potion

½ head Savoy or Napa cabbage,
  cut into small pieces

1 cup roughly chopped watercress

2 turns of a pepper mill

Pinch salt (optional)

MAKES 1 QUART

This is a true potion, rich in antioxidants and vitamins E, C, and B6. It is also a good source of zinc. Use it in small doses, as it is hard to take, but wonderful for you—cleansing, cooling, detoxifying, and rejuvenating. To make it even more healthful, add a little raw garlic.

Press the cabbage and watercress through the juicer and season with pepper and salt.

BRAZILIAN BLENDER JUICES

In Brazil, where fruit juices are a national treasure, most are made in a blender. Street-corner vendors mix mango, papaya, strawberries, and peaches with orange juice and ice. *Maracuja* (passion fruit) and *caju* (the fruit of the cashew tree) also play a large role in Brazilian fruit beverages. Should you have any fruit salad left from your Regime Cuisine breakfast, here is another great way to enjoy it. Purée the fruit combinations here with a few ice cubes to a thick consistency in a blender; each yields 1 quart.

ORANGE, PAPAYA, AND LIME

1½ cups diced peeled papaya
    (1 medium papaya)

2 cups orange juice

Juice of ½ lime

4 ice cubes

MANGO AND ORANGE

1 cup diced peeled mango
    (½ large mango)

½ banana

2½ cups orange juice

4 ice cubes

STRAWBERRY, PASSION FRUIT, AND PEACH

½ cup passion fruit juice

1 cup organic cranapple juice

1 cup orange juice

8 large strawberries

½ cup frozen peach slices

APPLE, MINT, AND MELON

½ cup orange juice

2 cups apple juice

2 cups melon chunks

8 mint leaves plus sprigs
    for garnish

4 ice cubes

PINEAPPLE, BANANA, AND CITRUS

2½ cups orange juice

1 cup finely chopped ripe
    pineapple

½ banana

4 ice cubes

HINTS: To extract the maximum amount of juice from citrus fruits, first heat them in a microwave oven for 30 to 40 seconds, then roll and press with the palm of your hand.

Try bottled cashew juice with the orange juice in the recipes.

REGIME CUISINE ESSENTIALS

BASIL PESTO

1½ pounds basil leaves, stems
    removed
¼ pound Italian parsley, stems
    removed
¾ cup olive oil
½ cup Vegetable Stock (page 166)
    or water
1½ teaspoons sea salt
½ teaspoon freshly ground pepper
8 cloves garlic, germs removed
¾ cup pine nuts
Olive oil

MAKES 2½ TO 3 CUPS

Combine the basil, parsley, oil, stock, salt, pepper, and garlic in a food processor or blender. Purée until smooth, taste, and adjust the seasoning as necessary. Add the pine nuts and continue to blend until they are uniformly chopped but not puréed.

Pour the mixture into containers and top with a film of oil to prevent oxidation and discoloration. Store up to 1 week, covered, in the refrigerator or freeze in small containers or ice cube trays.

SUNNY SALSA

Although this salsa is missing some of the heat of a Mexican salsa, its layered European flavors pack a punch. Serve this salsa with Baked Pita Crisps (page 75), sandwiches, pasta salads, and with grilled fish, chicken, and vegetables. (Pictured on page 77.)

2 red beefsteak tomatoes,
    roughly diced
1 yellow beefsteak tomato,
    roughly diced

½ yellow pepper, diced, blanched,
    and chilled
2 shallots, chopped
1 small clove garlic, minced
½ teaspoon lemon zest brunoise
    (page 102)
1 tablespoon virgin olive oil
1 tablespoon lemon juice
8 drops hot pepper sauce such as
    Tabasco
½ teaspoon anchovy paste
¼ teaspoon salt
8 to 10 turns of a pepper mill
1½ to 2 tablespoons tomato paste
15 basil leaves, cut into chiffonade

MAKES 2½ CUPS

Combine all the ingredients except the basil and tomato paste in a bowl and place it in the refrigerator for 15 to 20 minutes. Pour any excess liquid into a small bowl, add the tomato paste and mix together well to dissolve. Stir the tomato paste mixture into the salsa and fold in the basil leaves. The salsa will keep, covered, for 3 to 5 days in the refrigerator.

HINT: Tomato paste is used here to bind the ingredients together—use as little as possible.

SCENTED BASMATI RICE

Basmati cooked like this is great for cold dishes or can be reheated with a touch of olive oil in a nonstick pan. Try adding a pinch of saffron, a stalk of lemongrass, or a kaffir lime leaf to vary the flavors.

1 tablespoon olive oil
2 shallots, finely minced
2 cups basmati rice
2 strips lemon zest
1 small sprig rosemary
1 fresh bay leaf

4 turns of a pepper mill
¼ teaspoon Master Blend
    (page 167)
1 teaspoon salt

Heat a large saucepan over medium-high heat. Add the olive oil and shallots and cook just until the shallots are soft.

Add the rice and stir until it is lightly coated with the oil, then add 4 cups water. Bring to a boil, add the remaining ingredients, stir once, and cover. Reduce the heat to a simmer and cook for 5 minutes; remove the pan from the heat and set it aside for 5 minutes. Fluff the rice with a fork and turn it out into a shallow bowl to cool slightly.

RED WINE ONION COMPOTE

This compote is very low in fat. The olive oil is used only to add a sheen and to hold in the moisture. It is wonderful with meats and fish and adds a complexity to vegetable platters. A spoonful added to a plate of spice-crusted roasted lamb or duck will guarantee a memorable meal.

6 red onions, sliced
½ tablespoon cracked black pepper
½ tablespoon Master Blend
    (page 167)
½ tablespoon powdered ginger
¼ cup honey
½ bottle (about 1½ cups) red wine
    such as Burgundy or Zinfandel
2 tablespoons balsamic vinegar
Salt
½ tablespoon olive oil

MAKES 2 CUPS

Place the onions, pepper, Master Blend, ginger, honey, and wine in a stainless steel saucepan. Bring to a boil, then reduce the heat to a simmer. Cook until the onions are tender and most of the liquid has evaporated, about 45 minutes.

Remove from the heat and let the compote cool to room temperature. Season to taste with vinegar and salt and add the oil. The compote will keep, covered tightly, for 2 to 3 weeks in the refrigerator.

FENNEL AND WHITE WINE ONION COMPOTE

Fennel and fish have a reputation for going together. This compote is perfect for poached salmon, seared scallops, or roasted bass. But don't use it only with seafood—it's great with grilled turkey burgers and other meats too.

- 1 bulb fennel, thinly sliced
- 6 Vidalia onions, sliced (substitute other sweet onions if Vidalias are not in season)
- Freshly ground pepper
- 1/4 tablespoon crushed fennel seeds
- 1/4 tablespoon Master Blend (page 167)
- 2 tablespoons honey
- 1/2 bottle (about 1 1/2 cups) white wine such as Chablis
- About 2 tablespoons white vinegar
- Salt
- 1/2 tablespoon olive oil

MAKES 2 CUPS

Place the fennel, onions, 1/4 tablespoon pepper, the fennel seeds, Master Blend, honey, and wine in a stainless steel saucepan. Bring to a boil, then reduce the heat to a simmer. Cook until the fennel and onions are tender.

Remove from the heat and let the compote cool to room temperature. Season to taste with vinegar, salt and pepper and add the oil.

BASIC REGIME VINAIGRETTE

Most classic French vinaigrettes are one part vinegar to three parts oil. The oil is needed to calm the vinegar's bite. My recipe uses twice as much liquid as fat, and you won't miss the oil a bit. Use this vinaigrette on grilled vegetables, to marinate artichokes, and as a sauce over warm asparagus or steamed cauliflower. Several variations follow the basic recipe.

- 1/2 teaspoon Dijon mustard
- Juice of 1 lemon
- 1/2 cup good-quality sherry vinegar such as Xeres, or red wine vinegar or tarragon vinegar
- 1/4 cup Vegetable Stock (page 166) or water
- 1/4 cup olive oil
- Pinch crushed red pepper
- 10 turns of a pepper mill
- Pinch salt

MAKES APPROXIMATELY 1/2 CUP

Combine all the ingredients in a glass jar and shake vigorously. Open the jar, taste, and adjust the seasoning. Store in the refrigerator, but bring to room temperature before using.

Moroccan Vinaigrette
Replace the Vegetable Stock with orange juice and add orange zest brunoise (page 102) and mint to taste.

Vinaigrette aux Herbes
Use a grain mustard and add chopped tarragon, thyme, chervil, and chives.

Southwestern Vinaigrette
Add chili powder, minced jalapeño pepper or other fresh chilies, and chopped cilantro.

Thai Vinaigrette
Replace the lemon juice with lime and a little grated lime zest. Add a little fish sauce, Thai chilies, and a piece of crushed fresh lemongrass. Refrigerate overnight before using.

Golden Mustard Vinaigrette
Increase the amount of Dijon to 1 tablespoon and add 1 tablespoon pommery (grainy) mustard and chopped tarragon.

CURRY VINAIGRETTE

This power-packed sauce isn't just for salads. Try it over warm or cold poached chicken or fish. I also like to drizzle it over steamed vegetables and then serve them with herbed couscous for a light summer meal. You'll find dozens of other uses.

- 2 shallots, minced
- 1/2 clove garlic, minced
- 1/2 teaspoon grated fresh ginger
- 1 teaspoon honey
- 1 teaspoon curry powder
- Juice of 1 lemon
- 2 tablespoons tarragon vinegar
- 1/4 teaspoon salt
- 3 tablespoons olive oil
- 5 turns of a pepper mill

MAKES APPROXIMATELY 1/2 CUP

In a mixing bowl combine the shallots, garlic, ginger, honey, curry powder, lemon juice, vinegar, 1 tablespoon water, and salt. Mix well to blend the flavors, then add the oil and pepper and whisk energetically; taste and adjust the seasoning as necessary.

REGIME CREAMY VINAIGRETTES

These are creamy sauces for the 21st century. They are high in protein, low in fat, and they add richness and spice to chicken salads, Waldorf salads, chilled fish and meats, and sandwiches. They are also great on baked potatoes.

- 3/4 cup Regime Sour Cream (page 99)
- 1 teaspoon lemon zest brunoise (page 102)

1 tablespoon champagne vinegar

Juice of ½ lemon

5 drops hot pepper sauce such as
    Tabasco

Salt

Freshly ground pepper

MAKES APPROXIMATELY 1 CUP

Combine the Regime Sour Cream, lemon zest, vinegar, lemon juice, and hot pepper sauce. Mix well and season to taste with salt and pepper.

NOTE: You can make double or triple the recipe and divide it into batches and add a variety of flavorings.

Creamy Herb Vinaigrette
Add ¼ to ½ cup mixed chopped herbs such as tarragon, dill, chives, parsley, basil, and cilantro, and ¼ teaspoon minced garlic. Use tarragon vinegar.

Creamy Curry Vinaigrette
Add 1 teaspoon curry powder, ½ cup diced apple, and ¼ cup raisins. Use cider vinegar.

Creamy Chili Vinaigrette

Add a pinch of chili powder, 1 minced clove garlic, 2 tablespoons minced pickled jalapeño pepper, and ⅓ cup chopped cilantro. Use jalapeño juice in place of vinegar.

Creamy Green Mustard Vinaigrette
Add parsley juice (see Note), tarragon mustard, and fresh chopped tarragon. Use sherry vinegar.

NOTE: To make parsley juice, chop a bunch of parsley and place it in a piece of cheesecloth. Squeeze to release the juice. Squeezed parsley will keep longer than regular chopped parsley.

REGIME SOUR CREAM

Use this to replace either sour cream or mayonnaise. You won't feel guilty spreading this on sandwiches, dolloping it on baked potatoes, or using it in salad dressings and dips.

½ pound silken firm tofu (page 28)

½ pound extra-firm tofu (page 28),
    squeezed to remove excess water

Juice of 1 lemon

1 teaspoon honey

½ teaspoon salt

10 drops hot pepper sauce such as
    Tabasco

1 tablespoon safflower oil

MAKES APPROXIMATELY 2½ CUPS

Combine all the ingredients in a food processor or blender and purée until the mixture is smooth. Taste and adjust the seasoning as necessary. Pour into a container, cover tightly, and refrigerate. After storing, if water separates, pour it off and remix the sour cream in a blender. Regime Sour Cream will keep for 4 to 5 days in the refrigerator.

REFRIGERATOR JAM

As with everything in life, this jam is only as good as what you put into it. Because of their intense flavor I love to use small local strawberries. My other favorite flavors are plum, mango, pineapple, and mixed berry.

¼ cup honey

2 cups cleaned fruit (see Note)

¼ teaspoon Sweet Spices (page 167)

Small pinch salt

2 turns of a pepper mill

¼ teaspoon lemon zest brunoise

MAKES 1 CUP

Combine all the ingredients in a heavy-bottomed saucepan and bring to a boil.

Lower the heat and cook until the mixture is reduced by half.

TOFU CREAM CHEESE

I prefer this to the real thing: the taste is wonderful and the texture is light and smooth.

1 pound firm tofu (page 28),
    drained and gently squeezed to
    remove excess water

2 tablespoons white vinegar

Juice of ½ lemon

2 tablespoons safflower oil

¼ teaspoon salt

5 drops hot pepper sauce such as
    Tabasco

1 (7-gram) package powdered
    gelatin

MAKES 1 POUND

Combine the tofu, vinegar, lemon juice, oil, salt, and hot pepper sauce in a blender or food processor and purée until smooth. You will need to stop the blender and stir often with a spoon until the mixture is smooth.

Soak the gelatin in 1 tablespoon cold water, then heat it in a double boiler or in a measuring cup in a microwave oven until dissolved.

Pour the tofu mixture into a medium-sized mixing bowl and whisk in the gelatin. Place in an air-tight container and refrigerate for several hours before using. It will keep for 5 to 7 days.

HINT: Add a little more honey and some vanilla to make a great icing for zucchini or carrot cakes.

Overleaf, clockwise from top left:
Oranges in Red Wine; Roasted Poussins with
Truffles and Fava Beans; Grilled Butterfish;
Roasted Rhubarb and Figs with Orange;
Baby Bananas Foster; Spiced Tomato
Consommé with Summer Herbs.

DANIEL ORR

MENUS FOR ENTERTAINING

FROG LEGS SPICED WITH PICKLE MASALA, GARLIC, AND LEMON

3 cups flour

Salt

Freshly ground pepper

3 pounds cleaned imported frog legs, 16 to 18 legs per portion (see Note)

2 cups whole milk

About ¾ cup salad oil such as safflower

6 tablespoons unsalted butter

6 teaspoons chopped garlic

½ cup chopped Italian parsley

¼ teaspoon pickle masala (see Note)

Juice of 3 lemons

Tomato Compote (page 138)

Sautéed Zucchini (recipe follows)

Domestic frog legs—the ones most easily found—follow our bigger is better attitude, but if you can find the imported French ones, they're worth the extra cost. Serve bread to sop up the crunchy garlic bits and herb butter; finger bowls are a good idea if the party is dressy.

Season the flour with salt and pepper. Place the frog legs in the milk. Then with one hand remove them and squeeze gently to remove excess liquid; place the legs in the seasoned flour. With your dry hand, toss them in the flour until they are well coated, then remove them to a small tray. Flour only the number you are cooking at that time, or they will become soggy. For best results, use a pan large enough that the frog legs are not crowded. Do not cook more than 2 portions at one time in a 10-inch pan.

Place a pan with ¼ cup oil over high heat. When the oil is at the smoking point, carefully push about 2 portions of frog legs into the oil, using the tray as a safety shield to protect your hands. Quickly shake the pan to disperse the frog legs evenly and cook them until they are evenly crisp and brown, 5 to 7 minutes.

Using a large spatula as a guard, pour off and discard the excess oil. Return the pan to medium heat. Add 2 tablespoons butter and 2 teaspoons garlic and cook until the garlic begins to color slightly. Turn off the heat and add 2 tablespoons parsley and salt, pepper, and pickle masala to taste. Remove the frog legs to plates, and sprinkle them with freshly squeezed lemon juice. Continue with the remaining legs. Surround with the Tomato Compote and Sautéed Zucchini.

NOTES: If you use larger, domestic frog legs, plan 4 to 5 legs per portion.

Pickle masala brings out flavors without masking them and adds citrus acid notes.

SPICED TOMATO CONSOMMÉ WITH SUMMER HERBS

FOR THE CONSOMMÉ

1 tablespoon olive oil

3 onions, finely diced

5 cloves garlic, roughly chopped

8 pounds tomatoes, peeled, seeded, and roughly chopped (peels, seeds, and accumulated juices reserved)

1 gallon Vegetable Stock (page 166)

2 branches thyme

1 branch rosemary

2 fresh bay leaves

Salt

Freshly ground pepper

Hot pepper sauce such as Tabasco

FOR THE GARNISH

½ pint combination of red and yellow, round, cherry, and pear-shaped tomatoes

2 red beefsteak tomatoes, peeled, seeded, and cut into ¼-inch pieces

2 yellow beefsteak tomatoes, peeled, seeded, and cut into ¼-inch pieces

5 scallions, very thinly sliced

1 fresh Thai chili, very thinly sliced, seeds removed if you prefer less heat

Fresh herbs such as purple basil, green basil, cilantro, chives and chive flowers, dill and/or bronze fennel with flowers (the more variety the better)

This consommé is as wonderful chilled as it is piping hot. I vary the garnish with vegetables (paper-thin slices of small radishes add a contrasting color), herbs, and even shellfish or seafood sausage. Always add the garnish just before serving so it retains its vibrant color and the individual flavors sparkle through the acidic sweetness of the broth.

Heat the oil in a large stainless steel pot over medium-high heat. Add the onions and garlic and cook until they have released their moisture and softened but not browned, 5 to 7 minutes. Add the chopped tomatoes and stir well. Raise the heat to high and bring the mixture to a boil. Add the stock, thyme, rosemary, bay leaves, and the seeds, peels, and juice of the tomatoes, and return to a boil; season to taste with salt and pepper. Remove the pot from the heat and let the mixture steep for 10 minutes. Taste and season with salt, pepper, and hot pepper sauce as necessary. Strain the liquid through a colander, reserving the solids for another use, then strain it through several layers of rinsed cheesecloth in a strainer set over a large bowl. Let the consommé cool to room temperature. It will keep, covered, in the refrigerator for 3 to 5 days, or longer frozen.

Serve the consommé chilled, with the garnishes, in a large, chilled glass bowl.

NOTES: For smaller amounts of consommé, see the recipe for Tomato Compote (page 138).

For this recipe, choose the ripest, reddest tomatoes in the market. This really is a dish that can only be made in summer.

HINT: Making the consommé yields the basis for a second, terrific meal. The tomato solids are perfect for a ragout to be served with fish such as baked cod, or chicken or pasta. Simply add a couple tablespoons of tomato paste, a little olive oil, capers or pitted olives, fresh herbs, and plenty of freshly ground pepper.

GRILLED MEATS AND PEPPERS

For this casual dinner, marinate your meats several hours in advance or prepare them with rubs or pastes just before your guests arrive. If you have an assortment, plan to cut the meats up so that guests can sample each. For example, a sirloin steak or veal chop can be sliced into 6 or 8 pieces.

The most important part of grilling is knowing when your coals are ready. Whether you use briquettes or hard-wood charcoal, you must use plenty, burn them until they show a dusty white ash with a red-hot fire beneath, and cook close enough to the coals that heat sears and caramelizes the food. Use a heavy grid and preheat it to prevent sticking. The Red Wine Onion Compote (pages 97–98) and the Fennel and White Wine Onion Compote (page 98) are perfect with this meal.

The peppers can be cooked around the edge of the grill while the meat is at the center. Move them in while the meats are resting. This allows the peppers to cook through slowly and then get a final coloring. Cook them over medium heat, turning them every 2 to 3 minutes until all sides are lightly charred, 8 to 10 minutes. Season to taste with olive oil, salt, and pepper.

Assorted meats: Veal chops, steaks, squabs, quail, chicken, lamb, about 1 pound per person (seafood can be included)

For marinating: Vinaigrettes from *Regime Cuisine Essentials* (page 97) or *Real Food Basics* (page 160)

For grilling: Spicy Garlic Paste (page 162); Moroccan Pepper Sauce with Orange Zest (page 163); any of the Spice Blends (page 167) used as dry rubs

Assorted whole peppers: red, yellow, orange and green, including fresh hot peppers, Hungarian wax peppers, and banana peppers, 2 to 3 per person

Olive oil

Salt

Freshly ground pepper

BEET AND BEAN SALAD

Blanch the haricots verts and cranberry beans in separate pots of boiling water until tender, then chill them under cold water and drain.

Combine the haricots verts and beans with the Beet Salad and allow the salad to marinate for 2 to 3 hours in the refrigerator; toss to mix from time to time. Taste and adjust the seasoning just before serving. (Pictured on page 119.)

Beet and Red Onion Salad (page 39), fennel and fennel seeds omitted

½ pound haricots verts or young green beans

½ pound cranberry beans

HOBO POTATOES WITH PATTYPAN SQUASH

15 to 20 new, Red Bliss, or fingerling
  potatoes, sliced into ¼-inch rounds

10 baby pattypan squash, quartered

¼ cup olive oil plus additional

4 medium white onions, thinly sliced

4 cloves garlic, roughly chopped

2 teaspoons thyme leaves

Salt

Freshly ground pepper

This is one of the dishes that first sparked my interest in cooking. Summer Boy Scout campfires kindled my culinary spirit, along with lifelong friendships. Although I normally think of this recipe during July and August, these potatoes—if not the pattypans—are also great when cooked in the fireplace during the winter. For this number of servings, the dish must be made in 2 foil packages.

Blanch the potatoes in boiling water until they are half cooked, then chill them under cold water. Blanch the squash, then chill it under cold water.

Combine ¼ cup oil, the onions, and garlic with ¼ cup water in a medium-sized saucepan and cook until the onions are tender, 10 to 15 minutes. Add the thyme and season to taste with salt and pepper.

Toss the onion mixture, potatoes, and squash in a large bowl. Taste and adjust the seasoning.

Lay 2 double layers of aluminum foil shiny side down, and lightly oil the top surface.

Place half of the vegetable mixture on each double layer of foil, fold into packages, and seal well. If necessary, wrap an additional piece of foil around the packages. Place the packages around the edge of the fire, directly on the coals, while you are cooking the meats. Move the foil packages often so that the contents cook evenly. You will know how the cooking is progressing by the sound of the sizzling inside; cook for 15 to 20 minutes until the potatoes are tender.

Opposite: Grilled meats, Beet and Bean Salad, and Hobo Potatoes with Pattypan Squash.

DANIEL'S CHOCOLATE CAKE

¼ pound unsalted butter, plus
   additional for pan

4 ounces semisweet chocolate

⅔ cup sugar

3 extra-large eggs

6 ounces blanched almonds, ground to
   a powder

Grated zest of ½ orange

¼ cup very fine, fresh bread crumbs

Chocolate Glaze (recipe follows)

Almost flourless, this cake gives chocolate lovers a fix. Valrhona is the chocolate I prefer, but any top-quality chocolate will do.

Preheat the oven to 375° F.

Line the bottom of an 8-inch round cake pan with buttered parchment.

Melt the chocolate in a double boiler over simmering water.

Using an electric mixer cream the butter and gradually add the sugar, then the eggs one by one. The mixture will look curdled.

Fold in the remaining ingredients and the chocolate with a rubber spatula and pour the batter into the prepared pan. Bake for 20 to 25 minutes. The center should look somewhat underdone.

Cool the cake on a rack for 30 minutes, then turn it out of the pan onto a serving plate.

Pour the Chocolate Glaze over the cooled cake, filling in the cracks. Let the cake rest for 2 to 3 hours before serving, or refrigerate for 30 minutes. If the cake is refrigerated, remove it from the refrigerator 1 hour before serving.

HINT: This cake freezes well.

CHOCOLATE GLAZE

¾ cup heavy cream

8 ounces top-quality semisweet
   chocolate, chopped into small pieces

Bring the cream to a boil in a heavy saucepan, then remove it from the heat. Quickly add the chocolate and stir well to achieve a smooth consistency.

Allow the mixture to cool slightly before pouring it over the cooled cake.

HINTS: Use the glaze for dipping fruits for a chocolate fondue.

   Add a little more cream to leftover glaze to make a wonderful chocolate sauce; it can be finished with a couple of drops of Grand Marnier and served with the cake or with ice cream.

FRIDAY WITH FRIENDS

■

PASTA NOIR WITH CRAYFISH TAILS AND
RICE BEANS

BABY BANANAS FOSTER WITH
CARMELIZED ALMONDS

FOR SIX

Friends are always asking me to meet them for a bite before going to a movie, show, or nightclub. They think it's too much work to cook before going out. In rebuttal, I offer this two-course menu. It has elegance and simplicity, and when it's time to go you can slip the dirty pasta bowls into the cooking pot, squirt in a little soap, and leave them soaking. This menu is designed to be casual, with guests serving themselves buffet-style.

If crayfish or baby bananas are out of season, try substitutions such as scallops or shrimp for the pasta, and pineapple, large bananas, or green mango for the flaming Foster.

Baby Bananas Foster w/ Caramelized Almonds

A scoop of Ice cream

Flambéed Baby Bananas

Mint Sprig

The Caramelized Rum sauce

A sprinkle of crunchy Candied Almonds

PASTA NOIR WITH CRAYFISH TAILS AND RICE BEANS

½ cup rice beans (see Mail Order Sources, page 171), or other small white beans such as navy beans

1½ teaspoons plus 2 tablespoons sea salt

2 pounds live crayfish

Coarse sea salt

1½ pounds fresh squid-ink pasta

2 tablespoons olive oil

3 cloves garlic, chopped

1 tablespoon minced fresh ginger

⅓ cup dry white wine such as Chablis

½ cup clam juice or Fish Stock (page 165)

2 to 3 teaspoons julienned lemon zest

3 tablespoons lemon juice

1 pint heavy cream

10 turns of a pepper mill

1 pound cooked crayfish tails, or small shrimp or lobster meat cut into chunks

½ bunch cilantro, chopped, plus sprigs for garnish

Parmigiano-Reggiano cheese

Simple dishes need to be dramatic if your jaded friends are going to be impressed. I love the look of black pasta on a bright-colored platter. When the pasta is tossed with the red crayfish and white beans the contrasts are as beautiful as they are tasty.

Rinse the beans, place them in a pot with enough water to cover, and bring to a boil. Reduce the heat and simmer for 45 minutes. Add 1½ teaspoons sea salt and cook the beans until they are tender, about 15 minutes more. Allow the beans to cool in the water to room temperature, then drain and refrigerate until needed.

To clean the fresh crayfish, fan out the tail, grasp the center fin, twist, and pull out the vein. Place the crayfish on a baking sheet, sprinkle them with sea salt, and let them sit for 5 to 10 minutes; rinse under cold water.

In a 2-quart, heavy-bottomed, stainless steel pot, bring 1½ quarts water to a boil. Add 2 tablespoons salt and 1 tablespoon oil to the water and return it to a boil. Drop in the pasta and cook until it is al dente, 6 to 8 minutes; pay close attention as fresh pasta cooks very quickly. Pour the pasta into a strainer and rinse under hot running water to remove excess starch.

Following the instructions for steaming on page 168, steam the crayfish for 3 to 5 minutes, until they are cooked through.

Rinse the empty pasta pot and place it over medium-high heat. Add the garlic and the remaining oil and sauté until the garlic browns slightly. Quickly add the ginger, wine, clam juice, lemon zest, and lemon juice and bring to a boil; continue to cook until the liquid is reduced by half.

Add the cream to the sauce and bring it to a boil. Reduce the heat to a simmer and season with salt and the pepper. Return the pasta along with the beans to the pot, add the crayfish tails and cilantro, and toss to heat through. Pour the mixture into a warmed serving bowl and garnish it with cilantro sprigs and the steamed crayfish. Pass the cheese and a pepper mill at the table.

NOTE: Choose lively, fresh crayfish. Lobster heads and claw shells make a nice presentation when you are substituting its meat for the crayfish.

HINTS: Serve the pasta quickly after tossing it in the sauce; if it sits it will absorb sauce and become dry. If it does, add a few teaspoons of hot water or a little extra cream.

GARDENER'S VEGETABLE HORS D'OEUVRES

Baby eggplant

Artichokes

Pattypan squash

Baby zucchini and yellow squash

Assorted small tomatoes

Cipolline or other small onions

Regime Cuisine compotes (page 97–98), pestos, or chutneys

White Bean Purée (page 80)

Tomato Compote (page 138)

If you are lucky enough to have a garden plot to tend, and enjoy getting dirt under your nails, winter and early spring can be difficult. You long for the longer days of summer to give you time to toil with tasks that truly reward you with fruits of your labors.

I use tender homegrown baby vegetables as hors d'oeuvres, filling them with various condiments and even leftover compotes, pestos, and vegetables from previous meals. The idea for these comes from Nice's *petits farcies*, a regional Franco-Italian dish of vegetables filled with the season's bounty.

You can supplement the vegetables with crostini of crisp bread topped with salads or salsas, or with chips (lentil flour and black pepper Indian wafers are shown in the photo) topped with purées or chutneys.

Serve an assortment of warm and cold hors d'oeuvres chilled with cocktails in the garden or on the terrace, or present them on small plates for a more formal feel. Most of all, keep it seasonal and fresh!

Choose from the list of vegetables, planning on 5 pieces per person. Fill the vegetables with any of the suggested recipes from Regime Cuisine along with my Tomato Compote, which I like topped with a bit of grated cheese.

Cut the eggplant, squash, and onions in half and steam or blanch them until they are tender but still crisp. Chill them quickly in cold water to hold the color. Scoop out the centers to make cups for the fillings.

Cook the artichokes in boiling water until tender and carefully open them and scoop out the centers with a tiny spoon.

Cut off the tops of the tomatoes and gently squeeze out the seeds. Reserve the tops with greens to use as little *chapeaux*, and with a serrated knife, remove a sliver from the bottoms to keep the tomatoes from rolling.

BUTTERFISH GRILLED IN GRAPE LEAVES

12 whole butterfish, cleaned, heads and
  tails on, ½ pound each (see Choosing
  Fish and Shellfish, page 47)

Salt

Freshly ground pepper

12 basil leaves

6 thin lemon slices cut in half,
  plus 12 slices cut ⅛ inch thick

24 fresh grape leaves, or canned grape
  leaves, thoroughly rinsed

12 sprigs herbs such as sage, thyme,
  and rosemary, or a combination

Olive oil

I found these little fish for the first time in a vast Japanese fish market on the Upper East Side of New York. I later discovered that friends of mine use them for bait. What a waste! These fish are very meaty for their size and have a sweet, buttery flavor. The other good thing about them is they don't have scales and are easy to fillet after cooking. (Pictured on page 100.)

Prepare a charcoal fire.

Gut and rinse the butterfish and pat them dry with paper towels inside and out. Season with salt and pepper and fill the cavity of each fish with a half slice of lemon and a basil leaf.

On a cutting board or counter top, lay the grape leaves out in sets of 2 overlapping leaves. Place a butterfish on each set, letting a little of the head and tail hang out. Top with the herb sprigs and season with more salt and pepper. Drizzle with a little olive oil. Fold the leaves around the fish and top with the remaining lemon. Tie the wrapped fish and the lemon slices with butcher's twine.

Dip the packages in water to prevent the strings from burning.

When the coals are ready, grill the fish for approximately 5 minutes on each side. If the strings begin to burn, brush them with a little more water and move the fish to the side of the fire.

NOTE: Butterfish can be specially ordered from most fish markets, or you can substitute freshwater bluegill, or fillets of red snapper or black bass.

HINTS: Fish as well as fowl cooked in this manner take on the smoky, woody flavor of the grill and the moisture of the steam resulting from the leaf wrapping. Larger fish and pieces of meat can be wrapped in banana leaves.

I sometimes fill these fish with a little Tomato Compote (page 138) that I have accented with fresh herbs.

BLUEBERRY AND VANILLA PARFAIT WITH LEMON SORBET AND VERBENA

1 pint blueberries, washed well and frozen on a baking sheet

1 pint nonfat vanilla yogurt

1 pint lemon sorbet

1 tablespoon Candied Zest (pages 164–65; use only lemon zest)

6 sprigs lemon verbena

After working in the garden, cooking, and making witty conversation over dinner, who has the time or energy to bake a cake? Here is a simple, light dessert that is perfect on a hot summer evening.

Divide first the yogurt, then the blueberries in 2 layers each in tumbler glasses or glass bowls. Top each portion with lemon sorbet, candied zest, and a verbena sprig.

OUTDOOR ITALIAN BRUNCH

■

ANTIPASTO WITH ASSORTED MEATS, OLIVES, AND CHEESES

GRILLED GARLIC BREAD

FRITTATA OF SQUASH BLOSSOMS AND NEW POTATOES

SALAD TRICOLORE

TOASTED ALMOND GRANITA

FOR FOUR

A red and white tablecloth laid on the lawn is perfect for this al fresco meal. You won't need much more in the way of decoration.

Have the salad and the antipasto ready from the evening before. The granita can be made up to a week in advance and stored in a sealed container to be brought out at the last minute. Cook the frittatas in well-seasoned cast-iron pans over an open fire or on the grill, then quickly grill the bread.

Try a variation on a mimosa by using a slightly sweet Asti Spumante, an Italian sparkling wine, with grapefruit instead of orange juice—the balance of sweet and tart is quite nice. A light red wine or Italian mineral water are other good choices.

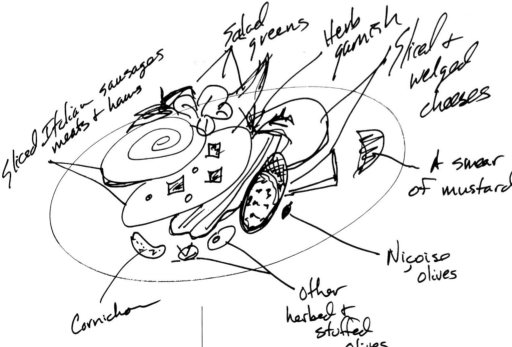

Sliced Antipasto with Assorted olives and Salad Tri-colori

Sliced Italian sausages meats & hams

Salad greens

Herb garnish

Sliced & wedged cheeses

A smear of mustard

Niçoise olives

other herbed & stuffed olives

Cornichon

ANTIPASTO WITH ASSORTED MEATS, OLIVES, AND CHEESES

¼ pound assorted meats per person

1 pound assorted olives

½ pound each of assorted Italian cheeses

I often marinate my own olives by draining them of their juice and tossing them with a dressing of olive oil, lemon juice, sliced garlic, rosemary, thyme, crushed red pepper flakes, and cracked black pepper. Other spices and herbs can be used, or drained pickled onions or gherkins added—use a variety of olives of different sizes, colors, and flavors.

Try to get imported prosciutto and have it sliced to order. Wrap it around chunks of mozzarella or shape it into roses. The platter can be arranged early in the day, covered with damp paper towels and then plastic wrap; remove it from the refrigerator an hour or two before serving. Roll slices of prosciutto around long, thin breadsticks at the last minute.

GRILLED GARLIC BREAD

12 (¾-inch) slices country bread

1 to 2 cloves garlic, cut in half

¼ cup extra-virgin olive oil

Coarse sea salt

Freshly ground pepper

My good friend Ralph Peratti, the chef and co-owner of Gabriel's in New York City, made these simple toasts for me over a backyard barbecue. I often use his method for crostini, croutons, or warm grilled vegetable and mozzarella sandwiches. The bread should be grilled just before serving. Don't leave it unattended, as it burns very quickly.

Prepare a charcoal fire. Place the slices of bread on the grid and grill them until crisp on both sides and well marked. Rub the garlic on one side of each slice, then brush them with oil and sprinkle with salt and pepper.

FRITTATA OF SQUASH BLOSSOMS AND NEW POTATOES

8 eggs

Coarse sea salt

Freshly ground pepper

1 tablespoon olive oil

4 to 6 new potatoes, thinly sliced into rounds

1 small onion, julienned

2 cloves garlic, roughly chopped

2 baby zucchini, thinly sliced into rounds

2 baby summer squash, thinly sliced into rounds

2 tablespoons chopped Italian parsley

1 teaspoon chopped rosemary

5 to 6 basil leaves, torn—not cut—into pieces

8 zucchini flowers (check to make sure they are bug free; open them and look inside)

¼ cup grated cheese such as Parmigiano-Reggiano, Gruyère, Cantal, or a mixture

Tomato Compote (page 138) or diced fresh tomatoes

Cracked black pepper

Chive blossoms and rosemary sprigs for garnish

In French an *omelette*, in Italian a *frittata*. Whatever the name, this dish is a perfect showcase for a bounty of squash blossoms, but when they are out of season, replace them with slices of blanched zucchini and summer squash. Japanese eggplant may also be used as a substitute or an additional ingredient that provides a meaty texture.

Preheat the broiler.

Whisk the eggs in a bowl and season with sea salt and pepper.

Heat an iron skillet, omelet pan, or nonstick sauté pan over medium heat and add the olive oil. Add the potatoes and onion and cook until the onion is soft and the potatoes begin to brown. Add the garlic, zucchini, and summer squash and cook until the squashes just begin to soften, 2 to 3 minutes—they need only to warm through. Season with salt and pepper and add the herbs.

Raise the heat to high, add the eggs, and gently toss them with the vegetables; cook until the eggs are slightly set but still very soft, then remove the pan from the heat.

With a spatula flatten the eggs and vegetables evenly in the pan and place the squash flowers in a pinwheel on top, pressing them gently into the egg mixture; sprinkle the top with the grated cheese.

Place the pan under the broiler and cook only enough to wilt, or collapse, the squash blossoms. Top the omelet with spoonfuls of Tomato Compote and a sprinkle of coarse sea salt and cracked pepper. Garnish with the chive blossoms and rosemary.

NOTE: If baby zucchini and summer squash are not available, use ¼ large zucchini, cut lengthwise then thinly sliced across.

SALAD TRICOLORE

The colors in this salad represent the Italian flag. Choose greens with different textures and flavors so each bite is exciting. Use red radicchio or red endive; white frisée, Belgian endive, or tender Bibb or Boston lettuce; and arugula, watercress, or spinach for the green. Set bottles of Italian olive oils and balsamic vinegar, a dish of sea salt, and a pepper grinder on the table and let your guests season their salads to their own tastes.

TOASTED ALMOND GRANITA

1 cup almond powder (blanched, ground almonds)

¾ cup granulated sugar

Juice of 1 orange

¼ teaspoon grated orange zest

1 cup almond syrup

2 tablespoons almond extract

1 cup marscapone (see Note)

2 tablespoons superfine sugar

¼ cup toasted sliced almonds

Mint sprigs for garnish

Combine the almond powder and granulated sugar in a small, heavy-bottomed saucepan over medium heat; cook until the sugar and almonds begin to caramelize. Quickly add 4 cups water, the orange juice, and orange zest and stir until the sugar is dissolved. Remove the pan from the heat and add the almond syrup and extract. Pour the mixture into a shallow, rectangular glass dish, let it cool to room temperature, then place in the freezer. Stir every 20 to 30 minutes until thick and slushy, then let it freeze solid.

Chill serving dishes. Allow the marscapone to sit at room temperature for 15 minutes before serving. Lightly whisk the marscapone together with the superfine sugar until the sugar dissolves.

Using a strong fork, scrape ice crystals from the frozen almond mixture and spoon it into the serving dishes. Accompany the ice with dollops of the whipped marscapone and garnish with the toasted almonds and mint sprigs.

NOTE: If marscapone is not available use crème fraîche or whipped cream.

HINT: Serve with assorted biscotti; chocolate ones contrast nicely with the almonds.

CITY SEAFOOD

■

SEARED SCALLOPS WITH TOMATO
COMPOTE AND BASIL OIL

CHILLED DOVER SOLE WITH
CAVIAR AND STROZZAPRETI

BRAISED DATES STUFFED WITH
FROZEN PISTACHIO CREAM,
WITH GRAPEFRUIT SALAD

FOR SIX

Spit-shine your shoes before the guests arrive for dinner: this is a menu for a dressier affair. The Tomato Compote and Basil Oil may be made several days in advance, and the falooda sev may be fried early in the afternoon and stored in an airtight container until needed. Even the scallops can be seasoned with everything except the sea salt, left on a plate in the refrigerator, and taken out several minutes before sautéing.

I serve the Dover sole chilled, making it perfect to do ahead of time, but it is equally good served warm in autumn or winter. Serve iced vodka in small, chilled glasses with the sole, or champagne throughout the meal—it's perfect with each dish and makes the meal a real celebration.

Dust off the good china and polish the silver. The extra effort will properly showcase the time you spent in the kitchen.

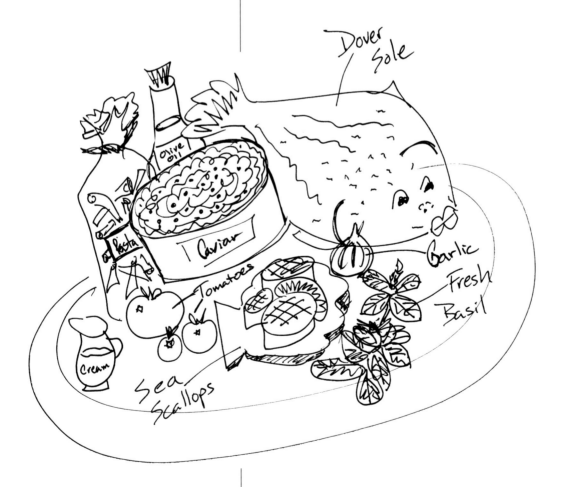

SEARED SCALLOPS WITH TOMATO COMPOTE AND BASIL OIL

Soybean oil for frying, plus 2
    tablespoons

4 ounces falooda sev (Indian yellow
    starch pasta) or Asian cellophane
    noodles

12 jumbo "dry" sea scallops (see Note)

1 tablespoon black cumin seeds

1/2 tablespoon sea salt

1/2 tablespoon cracked black pepper

1 tablespoon unsalted butter

1 cup Tomato Compote (recipe
    follows)

1/4 cup Basil Oil (recipe follows)

2 lemons, cut in half

8 green or purple basil leaves

The most important part of this recipe is the freshness of its ingredients. Scallops should have a sweet sea smell, not a fishy scent. Choose the ripest plum tomatoes, and select basil with an intense perfume.

Heat the soybean oil in a deep-fat fryer or a pan with 1/2 to 3/4 inch of oil, and fry the falooda sev for 20 seconds, until they stop bubbling. If using a pan, fry the noodles in small batches. Set aside on paper towels to drain.

Warm the Tomato Compote in a nonreactive saucepan over low heat; set aside in a warm place.

Remove the small, tough muscle from the sides of the scallops and gently rub them to feel for sand. If there is any sand, lightly rinse them, then dry them on paper towels.

Gently toss the scallops with the cumin, sea salt, and pepper in a small mixing bowl.

Heat a large, nonstick sauté pan over the highest possible heat. Add 2 tablespoons oil and the butter to the pan and cook just until the butter starts to brown. Place the scallops carefully in the pan and cook over high heat until the bottoms are crisp and caramelized, 2 to 3 minutes; avoid moving the scallops or they will release their juices and their flavor. Turn the scallops once and crisp and caramelize the other side. The scallops should be just warmed through and cooked medium-rare. (You can check by cutting one of the larger scallops in half and feeling the center; if it is cool, the scallops are underdone. If further cooking is needed, reduce the heat to medium-high and cook an additional minute or so.) Take care not to overcook the scallops, or they will become dry and tough.

Remove the scallops to a warm plate. Spoon a generous amount of Tomato

Compote into 4 scallop shells, or onto the centers of 4 warm appetizer plates. Place 3 scallops on each portion of compote and spoon a ring of the Basil Oil around. Squeeze lemon juice over each mound and top with the falooda sev and basil leaves.

NOTE: "Dry" scallops are the highest quality. They have been shucked but not processed. Diver's scallops are dry scallops that have been harvested by hand; they are generally available only to fine restaurants, but if you can find them, they are worth the extra expense.

35 very ripe plum tomatoes

1 sprig thyme

2 fresh bay leaves

1 sprig rosemary

¼ cup plus 3 tablespoons olive oil

10 shallots, minced

3 cloves garlic, minced

Salt

Freshly ground pepper

Hot pepper sauce such as Tabasco

MAKES APPROXIMATELY 1 QUART

TOMATO COMPOTE

Bring a large pot of water to a rapid boil. Fill a large bowl with cold water and ice. Trim away the stem end of the tomatoes and make a small X with a sharp knife at the other end. Plunge the tomatoes into the boiling water. After about 30 seconds, when the skin begins to loosen, drain the tomatoes in a colander then plunge them immediately into the ice water. When the tomatoes are completely cooled, in about 10 minutes, remove the skins; if you are making Tomato Consommé (see Hint), reserve the skins. Cut the tomatoes in half horizontally and gently squeeze them to remove the seeds; if you are making the consommé, reserve the seeds and juices.

Tie the thyme, bay leaves, and rosemary together with string.

Place a heavy-bottomed saucepan over medium heat. Add ¼ cup oil, the shallots, and garlic. After 1 minute add the bundle of herbs to the pan. Cook, stirring, until the garlic and shallots are tender, but not browned.

Place a shallow roasting pan over very high heat. Add the remaining olive oil to the pan, then quickly add the tomatoes and stir to sear them.

Add the shallot and garlic mixture and continue to cook until the mixture is heated through, but do not let it overcook; season to taste with salt, pepper, and hot pepper sauce.

Pour the mixture into a colander set in a mixing bowl and allow the liquid to drain into the bowl.

When the compote has drained and cooled to room temperature, pour it into a glass or plastic container, cover, and store in the refrigerator for up to 3 days. Save the reserved juices, seeds, and peels (see Hint).

HINT: A bonus from making the compote is a clear broth that can be used as a soup garnished with tender young vegetables and herbs, as a poaching liquid for fish, shellfish, or chicken, or to make ice cubes for Bloody Marys.

Bring the reserved juice to a boil. Add the skins and seeds, return to a boil, then remove from the heat. Set aside for 10 to 15 minutes.

Line a strainer with 3 layers of rinsed cheesecloth and place it over a container or bowl. Pass the broth through the strainer and season to taste with hot pepper sauce and salt.

BASIL OIL

1 tablespoon salt

½ bunch Italian parsley, leaves only, washed

2 large bunches basil, leaves only, washed

½ tablespoon finely chopped garlic

2 cups extra-virgin olive oil

½ tablespoon sea salt

1 teaspoon freshly ground white pepper

MAKES 3 CUPS

Bring ½ gallon water and the salt to a boil.

Add the parsley and cook for 2 minutes, then add the basil and cook an additional 30 seconds. Immediately pour into a strainer and press out all the excess water.

Place the garlic, 1½ cups oil, the sea salt, white pepper, and the blanched herbs in a blender. Process at high speed until the purée is very fine. Taste and adjust the seasoning with salt and pepper as necessary. Pour the mixture into a glass jar or container and top with the remaining oil. Place ice cubes and water in a mixing bowl; immediately place the jar of oil into the bowl to preserve the color. The flavor of the oil will develop 2 to 3 hours after blending. Store the oil for 2 to 3 days in the refrigerator or up to 3 months in the freezer. Mix well before using.

CHILLED DOVER SOLE WITH CAVIAR AND STROZZAPRETI

Salt

1 pound fresh strozzapreti pasta or
   dried penne or orecchiette

2 tablespoons olive oil

Freshly ground pepper

6 branches thyme

6 (1-pound) Dover sole, heads
   removed, skinned and gutted,
   but left on the bone

6 shallots, thinly sliced

2 cups dry white wine

1 quart Fish Stock (page 165), or
   1 pint clam juice and 1 pint water

2 teaspoons sea salt

2 fresh bay leaves

10 white peppercorns, crushed

½ stalk lemongrass, cut in half
   lengthwise

2 lemons, thinly sliced

1 pint heavy cream

Hot pepper sauce such as Tabasco

1 teaspoon lemon zest brunoise
   (page 102)

Juice of 2 lemons

2 tablespoons chopped chives

2 tablespoons chopped fennel tops
   or dill

1 teaspoon finely cracked black pepper

Flat fish such as turbot and Dover sole are among the finest, most delicate tasting in the world. Others like brill, flounder, and lemon and gray sole are flakier and less elegant, but often can be substituted. I like this dish because it can be made in advance and put together at the last minute. It also is wonderful made just before serving and eaten slightly warm.

Bring a large pot of lightly salted water to a boil. Drop in the pasta and cook until it is al dente; drain and rinse under cold running water to chill. Toss the pasta with 1 tablespoon oil and salt and pepper to taste; place in the refrigerator.

Coat the bottom of a large, shallow roasting pan with 1 tablespoon oil. Place the thyme branches in the pan, spacing them so there will be one under each sole. Season the sole on both sides with salt and pepper and place them on the thyme in a single layer in the pan. (Use two pans if you don't have one large enough.) Scatter the shallots over the fish and pour in the wine and fish stock to cover. Scatter the sea salt, bay leaves, peppercorns, lemongrass, and lemon slices over.

Place the pan over medium heat, bring to a low boil, then lower the heat to keep it at a simmer. After about 5 minutes, turn the fish and cook for 5 minutes more. Remove the pan from the heat and allow the fish to cool slightly in the broth for 8 to 10 minutes. Carefully remove the sole to a baking sheet. Fillet the fish by running a spatula or knife down the center of each fish, following the natural split, then carefully lift each fillet off the bones. Turn the fish and remove the two remaining fillets.

Place the fillets in their original pairs in a dish, ladle in a little of the broth to cover the fillets, and cover the dish tightly with plastic wrap. Refrigerate until serving.

4 tablespoons extra-virgin olive oil

2 ounces caviar (sevruga, osetra, beluga, American, or salmon or trout roe)

Fennel tops, dill sprigs, or chives for garnish

Just before serving, whip the cream in a large mixing bowl until it is frothy and light, but not firm. Season to taste with salt, pepper and 2 or 3 drops hot pepper sauce.

Toss the pasta in another bowl with the lemon zest, half the lemon juice, the chives, half the fennel tops, and cracked pepper; season with salt. Add the pasta to the whipped cream and gently toss to coat; adjust the seasoning.

Combine the extra-virgin olive oil and the remaining lemon juice in a small bowl and season to taste with salt and pepper.

Divide the pasta among 6 chilled serving plates, top each portion with 4 fillets, and spoon the lemon dressing over the pasta. Garnish with the caviar, chives, and remaining fennel tops.

NOTE: Poached salmon or char can be substituted for the sole.

HINT: If serving this dish warm, spoon the cream sauce over the warm pasta at the last minute, as the foam will quickly liquefy.

BRAISED DATES STUFFED WITH FROZEN PISTACHIO CREAM, WITH GRAPEFRUIT SALAD

30 Madjol dates

3 cups white wine such as Chardonnay

¼ cup sugar

1 cup honey

½ teaspoon saffron threads

2 pieces star anise

1 stick cinnamon

5 cloves

1 teaspoon Master Blend (page 167)

5 strips lemon zest

Juice of 1 lemon

1 pint pistachio ice cream

¼ cup chopped pistachios

2 pink grapefruits, cut into segments, membranes removed

20 mint leaves, cut into chiffonade

Juice of 2 limes

Pinch saffron threads

6 sprigs mint for garnish

Here, the bittersweet, acid grapefruit is the perfect foil for the creamy richness of the ice cream and sunny sweetness of the dates. (Pictured on page 7.)

Begin several hours before serving. Pit the dates by cutting a slit the long way down each and carefully squeezing the two ends to open them up. Remove and discard the pits.

In a medium-sized saucepan combine the wine, sugar, honey, ½ teaspoon saffron, the star anise, cinnamon, cloves, Master Blend, lemon zest and juice, and 1 cup water. Bring to a boil and stir to dissolve the honey and sugar. Reduce the heat to a simmer and add the dates; remove the pan from the heat and set aside to cool to room temperature, then refrigerate.

Remove the dates from the syrup with a slotted spoon and lay them out on a small tray with the open sides up. Place a small oval scoop of ice cream in each one and sprinkle with chopped pistachios. Gently press the dates closed and place in the freezer.

Toss the grapefruit segments with the chiffonaded mint and 2 to 3 spoonsful of the syrup.

Strain the remaining syrup into a saucepan over medium heat and cook until it is reduced to 1½ cups. Squeeze in the lime juice and add the saffron threads.

To serve, place the grapefruit salad in the centers of 6 chilled dessert plates, surround with 5 dates each, and garnish with mint sprigs. Reheat the sauce and spoon it around each date; serve immediately.

HINT: Leftover syrup may be reheated and spooned over fresh berries.

MEET ME ON THE ROOF

■

JUMBO SHRIMP WITH TWO ASPARAGUS
"MER ET TERRE" SALAD

ORANGES IN RED WINE

FOR TWO

City folks have always climbed to the roof to get away from the kids, neighbors, and the summer heat, and for the romantic views of sunsets and Fourth of July fireworks. No matter what the reason, a little grub will allow you to "hold out" a little longer.

This menu is designed as a romantic escape for two. It is uncomplicated and is meant to enhance the viewing and the conversation—not overpower them. The meal is easy to carry up on a tray or in a basket, and silverware isn't needed—shrimp and asparagus can be dipped in the vinaigrette, and the oranges eaten with your hands.

I use old silver ocean-liner bowls filled with a little crushed ice for the "Mer et Terre" salad, but it is just as nice served from a single larger bowl. Of course, champagne glasses are appropriate, but I've been known to down-scale to plastic for more adventurous rooftop rendezvous.

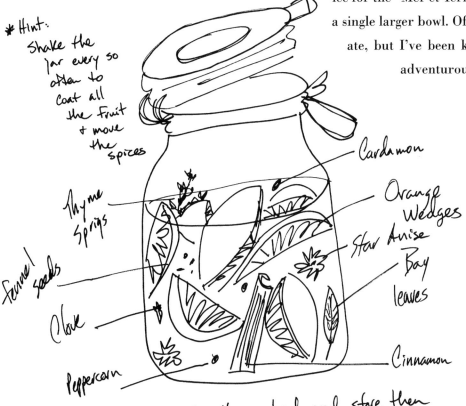

* Hint: shake the jar every so often to coat all the fruit + move the spices

Cardamon

Orange Wedges

Star Anise

Bay leaves

Cinnamon

Thyme Sprigs

Fennel Seeds

Clove

Peppercorn

* Note: I like to make these ahead and store them in resealable jars so I can pack them in my picnic basket!

JUMBO SHRIMP WITH TWO ASPARAGUS "MER ET TERRE" SALAD

10 spears jumbo white asparagus

10 spears jumbo green asparagus

Seafood Nage (pages 165–66)

16 jumbo shrimp, unpeeled

¼ pound pousse pierre, sea beans (fresh if possible), or haricots verts

6 pickled hot peppers

6 to 8 pea shoots, or watercress stems

Mustard Herb Sauce (page 162)

Spicy Pink Sauce (page 162)

This is finger food at the highest level and proves that elegance is not defined by multiple sets of silverware. Whether for a rooftop dinner or a country picnic, this do-ahead dish will satisfy. Vary the vegetables and dipping sauces to your own taste—I often use Regime Cuisine dips (pages 76–78).

If they are very fibrous, scrape the asparagus with a vegetable peeler from the tip down.

Place a large pot of water over high heat and bring to a boil; add a pinch of salt and the asparagus and cook until the asparagus are tender but still crisp, 6 to 8 minutes. Take care not to overcook the asparagus. Drain the asparagus, reserving the cooking water, and plunge them into a bowl of ice water to chill quickly. Remove the asparagus spears from the ice bath as soon as they are cold, or they will become waterlogged and limp. Wrap the asparagus in a cloth towel and place in the refrigerator; they can be kept for up to 2 days.

Bring the nage to a boil, add the shrimp, and return the broth to a simmer; simmer for 2 to 3 minutes until the shrimp are just cooked through—do not overcook them. Remove the shrimp to a bowl with a few ice cubes to stop the cooking and reserve the broth for another use.

Return the asparagus water to a boil. Add the pousse pierre and blanch them for 1 minute. Immediately plunge them into ice water until they are cold, 2 to 3 minutes; keep in the refrigerator until needed.

To serve, place crushed ice on a platter or tray. Arrange the shrimp, asparagus, pousse pierre, pickled peppers, and pea shoots over the ice. Serve immediately with bowls of the sauces for dipping.

HINTS: To test the fibrousness of green or white asparagus, break one in half. If it does not snap readily, it will need peeling. Some cooks simply discard the stem from below the point that it will easily snap. White asparagus tend to have tough fibers.

If you cook the shrimp in advance, chill the nage, then spoon some of it over the shrimp in the storage container—this will help to keep it moist.

¼ cup white raisins

¼ cup black raisins

½ cup brandy

1¼ to 1½ pounds foie gras, grade B
   (see Hint)

1 teaspoon cracked black pepper

1 teaspoon coarse sea salt

1 teaspoon Master Blend (page 167)

Flour for dredging

¾ cup Red Wine Sauce (page 163) or
   duck or veal glaze

1 tablespoon salad oil such as safflower

2 to 3 tablespoons balsamic vinegar

30 green grapes

30 small red grapes

30 champagne grapes

2 tablespoons cold unsalted butter

Pinch coarse sea salt

12 sprigs chervil

SAUTÉED FOIE GRAS WITH FRESH "RAISINS"

One of my mental blocks when cooking in the kitchens of several of the great restaurants of France was the word *raisins*. Each time I was told to get them I would go to the dry storeroom for the shriveled dried grapes, not the fresh ones the chefs were looking for. In this recipe, I've used both.

Cooking foie gras is relatively simple, but at over 45 dollars a pound, you don't want to make any mistakes. What makes hot foie gras special is the interplay of a crisp exterior crust and a melt-in-your-mouth interior. Coating the slices of well-chilled liver, then cooking it in a very small amount of oil in a heavy-bottomed pan over high heat is part of the secret. A heavy pan is important because it holds the heat when the chilled liver hits the pan; a thinner pan will cool, and the liver will release some fat.

The other important aspect is not to overcook the liver, either by burning it or cooking it too long. Because of the high temperature, you must work quickly to sear the first side and turn it over. I usually remove the pan from direct heat to cook the second side a little more slowly, until it is just colored and the interior has lost its firmness and is warmed through. Foie gras usually becomes overcooked when the pan is too light or the flame too low. Then, liver loses too much of its golden fat and becomes tough, dry, and tastes like, well, liver!

Above all, speed is most important. You must work quickly with foie gras or it becomes flabby and unappetizing. Be organized, completely set up and ready to serve. Have your guests seated and the wine poured before you cook the liver. Otherwise, you might as well serve liver and onions.

The richness of foie gras needs to be balanced by its accompaniments. I usually do this with slightly sweet or acidic ingredients such as the balsamic vinegar and grapes in this recipe. I also like woodsy or earthy flavors with foie gras such as wild mushrooms and root vegetables.

Then, I decrease the acidity of the sauce to let the more subtle flavor shine through and let the wine or port I serve with the foie gras bring tannic, acid, and sweet notes to the experience.

In a small saucepan over very low heat, soak the raisins in ½ cup water and the brandy until the raisins are plump and tender, about 30 minutes.

Separate the foie gras into its two lobes by gently pulling them apart. Remove the excess fat that separates the two lobes. Carefully cut the foie gras into 12 (½-inch-thick) slices as equally as possible. Gently press the thicker pieces with the palm of your hand to make all the slices of equal thickness. Season both sides of the pieces with the pepper, sea salt, and Master Blend, then

(continued)

dredge them in the flour. (The cutting and seasoning can be done up to 5 hours in advance, and the slices dredged just before cooking.)

Wash the grapes and cut the red and white grapes in half. Warm the Red Wine Sauce in a small saucepan. Place the serving plates in a very low oven to warm.

Heat a heavy-bottomed skillet, preferably cast-iron, over high heat; the skillet should be just large enough to hold the foie gras comfortably.

Add the salad oil, followed quickly by the foie gras. Brown on the first side and turn, reduce the heat to medium, and cook the foie gras until it is just warmed through and crisp on the outside. Remove the foie gras from the pan with a slotted spatula and place it on paper towels on a warm plate; set aside in a warm place.

Working quickly, pour off the fat from the pan, reserving it for another use. Deglaze the pan with the vinegar and return it to high heat. Add the grapes, raisins, and the sauce. Bring the sauce to a boil and cook until it is reduced to a syrupy consistency, 2 to 3 minutes. Add the butter and swirl the pan to incorporate it.

Place the foie gras on the serving plates, pat with a paper towel to absorb excess fat, and spoon the raisin sauce over. Sprinkle with several grains of coarse sea salt, garnish with the chervil sprigs, and serve immediately.

HINTS: Use foie gras graded A for cold terrines and the meatier grade B for hot dishes.

Always save the fat that is exuded during the cooking of the foie gras. It is wonderful for sautéing baby spinach or to add at the end when sautéing potatoes. I also use it in warm vinaigrette or even on baked potatoes in place of butter. If the fat has a lot of brown specks in it, strain it into a jar while warm and allow them to settle, then use the clear part that rises to the top. The fat freezes well.

This dish can be served over a bed of sautéed baby spinach or with a few leaves of mâche and frisée.

Keep a jar of the plumped raisins in the refrigerator; they are great with pork, fruit, oatmeal, or ice cream.

ROASTED POUSSINS WITH TRUFFLES AND FAVA BEANS

1 cup shelled fava beans (1 pound unshelled)

Salt

1 pound dried orecchiete pasta

2 ounces fresh black truffles, summer truffles, or wild mushrooms, gently scrubbed in warm water

3 tablespoons plus 1 teaspoon olive oil

1 teaspoon chopped garlic

1½ cups Chicken Stock (page 166)

¾ pound truffle butter, or mushroom butter (see Note), at room temperature or cold

1 teaspoon lemon zest brunoise (page 102)

Freshly ground pepper

¼ cup roughly chopped Italian parsley

6 (14- to 16-ounce) poussins

Stuffed Pattypan Squash (recipe follows)

Thyme sprigs for garnish

Garlic Confit (page 164)

Sea salt

P oussins are tender young chickens. Their mildness makes them perfect vehicles for the earthy flavor of the truffles—you'll be picking up the bones to savor every last bite. If you have them use your finger bowls. The fava beans and pasta can be prepared the day before and reheated in the poussin pan at the last minute. (Pictured on page 100.)

To remove the skins from the shelled fava beans, plunge them into boiling salted water for 1 minute, drain, and refresh under cold water. Split the beans with your thumbnail and squeeze out the tender, bright green fava. Discard the tough outer shell.

Bring a large pot of water to a boil. Add a pinch of salt and the pasta and cook until the pasta is al dente, about 12 minutes. Drain in a colander.

Slice the truffles into thin rounds. Save the 12 most perfect slices and cut the rest into julienne; reserve the slices.

Heat 1 teaspoon oil in a large saucepan over medium-high heat, add the garlic, and sauté until it is just lightly browned. Pour in 1 cup stock and cook to reduce it by half. Add the pasta and fava beans and heat them through. Stir in ¼ pound truffle butter, the lemon zest, and the julienned truffles. Season to taste with salt and pepper, sprinkle with parsley; remove from the heat.

Preheat the oven to 475° F.

Rinse and pat dry the poussins, inside and out. Carefully loosen the skin of the birds by running your thumb under at the point of the breastbone, and continue without tearing until you reach the neck. Set the chickens aside.

Slide one slice of truffle under the skin of each breast; push in a little salt and pepper. Put the remaining room-temperature truffle butter into a pastry bag or cut cold butter into thin pieces. Divide the butter amongst the birds, placing it under the skin. Truss the birds with twine.

(continued)

Heat a 12-inch nonstick pan with an ovenproof handle over high heat. Season the poussins with salt and pepper. Pour 3 tablespoons oil into the pan and carefully follow with the birds, thigh side down. Cover the pan loosely with aluminum foil, cook until the birds are brown, 3 to 4 minutes, then turn them onto their backs. Remove the foil, place the pan in the oven, and cook for about 15 minutes or until the thigh juices run clear.

Remove the poussins to a warm platter and cover loosely with aluminum foil.

With a paper towel wipe any excess fat from the pan that the poussins were in. Deglaze the pan with ½ cup stock, season to taste with salt and pepper, pour in the pasta, and cook to heat through.

To serve, place the stuffed pattypans on a large platter. Follow with half the pasta, then the poussins. Spoon on the remaining pasta to add height and fill in any gaps. Garnish the platter with thyme sprigs, whole heads of garlic confit, and a sprinkle of sea salt.

NOTES: If you can't find truffle butter, 1 cup softened butter can be seasoned with finely chopped sautéed and cooled wild mushrooms, grated lemon zest, minced garlic, chopped shallots, chopped fresh thyme, and salt and pepper; a drizzle of white truffle oil will boost the flavor.

Cornish hens or squabs can be substituted; cook squabs to medium-rare.

Stuffed Pattypan Squash

Bring a pot of water to a boil. Add the squash and cook until they are three-quarters cooked, 5 to 7 minutes. Drain and cool the squash under cold running water. Trim the bottoms if necessary to level; cut off the tops and reserve. Scoop out the flesh and seeds, leaving a ¼-inch shell; season the squash with salt and pepper. Combine the compote and the herbs; fill the squash with the mixture and cover with the tops. (This may be done up to 24 hours in advance.)

Place the squash in a baking dish and pour in water to cover the bottom. Put the squash in the oven for the last 15 minutes of cooking the poussins.

6 medium (2½- to 3-inch) pattypan squash

2 cups Tomato Compote (page 138)

½ cup chopped fresh herbs such as tarragon, chives, basil, and sage

RHUBARB CONSOMMÉ WITH STRAWBERRIES, MINT, AND RHUBARB SORBET

5 pounds rhubarb, leaves removed and discarded, roughly chopped

4 cups dry white wine

1 vanilla bean, split lengthwise

3 cups sugar

2 sticks cinnamon

¼-inch slice fresh ginger, cut on a bias

1½ pints strawberries, sliced and chilled

10 to 15 mint leaves, cut into chiffonade

1 tablespoon Candied Zest (pages 164–65; use only orange zest)

Rhubarb Sorbet (recipe follows)

3 sprigs mint

It amazes me every time someone asks me, "What exactly is rhubarb?" My stock answer is that it looks like red celery. Rhubarb always reminds me of my childhood and the warnings of my mother that its leaves were poisonous—it was sort of the blowfish of the vegetable world. I guess that intrigued me, for now rhubarb is one of my favorite vegetables, with the sweet and acid tones of berries, peaches, and honey that set off its sour notes. Here, its complexity is accented by mint and strawberries.

(continued)

In a large saucepan place the rhubarb, wine, vanilla bean, sugar, cinnamon, and ginger and bring to a boil. Reduce the heat to a simmer and cook for 10 to 12 minutes until the rhubarb has released its juices. Remove the pan from the heat and let the mixture steep for 10 to 15 minutes. Pour the liquid through a strainer and reserve the solids for the rhubarb sorbet. (The syrup may be prepared up to 2 days in advance or frozen for up to a month.)

Just before serving (not more than 1 hour in advance), place the cold strawberries in a metal bowl set over another bowl with ice. Reheat the syrup in a saucepan until it is just warm, pour the syrup over the berries, then set aside to cool. Add the chiffonaded mint and Candied Zest.

To serve, ladle the syrup and berries into individual bowls and add a scoop of Rhubarb Sorbet; garnish with the mint sprigs.

NOTE: Precut frozen rhubarb can be used if fresh rhubarb is out of season.

RHUBARB SORBET

3 cups chopped fresh rhubarb, or 2 cups of the solids from the Rhubarb Consommé (preceding recipe)

1 cup white wine such as Chardonnay

1 cup sugar

Juice of 1 orange

Juice of 1 lemon

1 teaspoon ground cinnamon

1 vanilla bean, split lengthwise and scraped to remove the seeds

1 teaspoon orange zest brunoise (page 102)

Heat the rhubarb, wine, sugar, and 1 cup water in a medium-sized saucepan over medium heat and bring to a boil. Lower the heat to a simmer and cook until the rhubarb is tender and the sugar is dissolved, 8 to 10 minutes.

Remove the pan from the heat and add the orange and lemon juices, cinnamon, vanilla pod and seeds, and orange zest, and allow them to steep until the liquid comes to room temperature.

Remove the vanilla pod. Purée the mixture in a blender or with a hand mixer until it is smooth, then pass it through a fine sieve.

Freeze the purée in an ice-cream machine as directed by the manufacturer.

DINNER ON THE CÔTE D'AZUR

■

CHILLED CURRIED CARROT SOUP
WITH ORANGE

ROASTED STRIPED BASS WITH
BABY ARTICHOKES AND
OLIVE-VEGETABLE RAGOUT

POACHED PURPLE AND YELLOW PLUMS
WITH LAVENDER SORBET

FOR SIX

The cuisine of the French Riviera is essentially Provençal food in eveningwear. The bold, honest flavors have been refined a bit, an approach that should be followed in the presentation of the meal and in the table decoration; I use lots of white, accented by shades of blue. This is a wonderful menu to serve al fresco, and it is equally good at lunch.

To start, offer a pastis with plenty of water and a few ice cubes to set the French mood. Then, the chilled dry rosés that are favorite summer lunch wines in the south of France are perfect. Finish the meal with strong coffee and good brandy.

The carrot soup may be served warm during the cooler months when a little extra curry has a soul-warming effect. Make the soup several days in advance, then poach the plums and freeze the sorbet the evening before you will be serving it. Several hours before the guests arrive, prepare everything for the bass, and finish it while friends are clearing the soup bowls and pouring more wine. Serve the fish right out of the oven or off the grill. Place several saltcellars filled with coarse gray sea salt around the table.

Chilled Carrot and orange Soup w/ Curry and whipped saffron Cream

chive batonette

Swirl of saffron cream

the diced carrots

The soup

Could be dramatic with some pumpernickle crisps (see regione cuisine)

DANIEL ORR REAL FOOD   155

CHILLED CURRIED CARROT SOUP WITH ORANGE

FOR THE SOUP

14 carrots, scraped

1 bulb fennel

1 onion, finely chopped

2 cloves garlic, minced

3 sprigs thyme

2 bay leaves

Juice of 1 orange

Zest of ½ orange, cut into brunoise
  (page 102)

1½ teaspoons Mellow Yellow (page
  167) or Madras curry powder

½ teaspoon ground turmeric

2 tablespoons coarse sea salt

1 tablespoon honey

2 quarts Chicken or Vegetable Stock
  (page 166), or water

Salt

Freshly ground pepper

1 cup heavy cream

¼ bunch chives, cut into ¾-inch lengths

FOR THE SAFFRON CREAM

1 tablespoon saffron threads

½ cup crème fraîche

Salt and freshly ground pepper

¼ teaspoon lemon zest brunoise
  (page 102)

Choose fresh carrots with their tops still attached, which usually are the freshest—their sweetness will be both enhanced and transformed by the curry and orange, taking them where no carrot has been before. A sunny day, a turquoise-blue swimming pool, and a bowl of this soup and you'll transport yourself, if not to Cannes, then somewhere better.

Put 10 carrots and the remaining soup ingredients except the cream, salt, pepper, and chives in a stainless steel pot, bring to a simmer, and cook until the carrots are soft, 25 to 30 minutes. Purée the soup in a blender or food processor until smooth, then pass the purée through a fine strainer into the pot. Season with salt and pepper to taste, add the cream, return the liquid just to a boil, then remove the pot from the heat and let the soup cool to room temperature. Place in the refrigerator to chill thoroughly.

Dice the remaining carrots and blanch them in boiling water until tender, 3 to 4 minutes. Drain and refresh under cold water to chill.

Crush the saffron between your fingers and place in a small bowl. Bring 2 tablespoons water to a boil, pour it over the saffron, and set aside to steep for 10 to 15 minutes.

Put the crème fraîche in a small bowl, add the saffron water, and lightly whip to combine. Season to taste with salt, pepper, and lemon zest.

To serve, ladle the soup into chilled bowls. Spoon a swirl of saffron cream on top and garnish with the diced carrots and the chives.

ROASTED STRIPED BASS WITH BABY ARTICHOKES AND OLIVE-VEGETABLE RAGOUT

3 (2½-pound) striped bass; or 6 (5½- to 6-ounce) bass fillets

Several branches thyme or rosemary, or fennel tops

6 cloves garlic, thinly sliced

18 fresh baby artichokes or commercial canned artichoke hearts

2 large yellow tomatoes, roughly chopped

2 red beefsteak tomatoes, chopped

1 fresh red Thai chili pepper, seeds and veins removed, finely diced

3 fresh bay leaves

30 to 40 Niçoise olives

6 to 8 strips lemon zest made with a vegetable peeler

18 pearl onions, peeled and blanched

1 cup roughly chopped basil

1 bunch chives, roughly chopped

½ cup extra-virgin olive oil

2 to 3 tablespoons coarse sea salt

2 to 3 tablespoons Mixed Pepper Blend (page 167)

Fresh herb sprigs for garnish

Garlic Confit (page 164), warmed

2 to 3 lemons, cut in half

Roasting on the bone increases the flavor and moisture of the meat; and when the dish is brought to the table, it gives your guests a sense of communal well-being—the sense that you will be sharing something, much like the breaking of bread. If you've never cooked a whole fish, try this first with with a 2½-pound striped bass, snapper, bluefish, or black sea bass for two. However, fish fillets or steaks may be used in place of whole fish. The olive and vegetable ragout goes with almost any fish.

Place a large roasting pan (or 2 smaller pans on separate racks) in the oven and preheat the oven to 500° F.

Pat the fish dry with a paper towel and fill the cavities with herb branches and several pieces of the sliced garlic; set aside.

Remove the tough exterior leaves and the stems from the artichokes and cut

off the pointed tops. Cook the artichokes in boiling water until they are tender but not mushy, about 15 minutes. Drain and shock them under cold water to stop the cooking; cut them in half lengthwise.

Have the tomatoes, artichokes, chili, bay leaves, olives, lemon zest, onions, basil, and chives ready on a platter to be added as soon as the fish is removed from the pan.

Coat the fish very lightly with oil, season both sides with sea salt and the Mixed Pepper Blend. Pour the remaining oil into the roasting pan. When the oil reaches the smoke point, carefully place the fish in the pan, laying it away from you, so the oil will not splash back at you.

Quickly close the oven so that heat does not escape. Cook the fish for 8 to 10 minutes (for a 2½- to 3-pound fish), then turn it over with a large spatula (again, turn it away from you), and cook for 5 to 7 minutes more. To test for doneness, insert a sharp knife point into the thickest part of the fillet and cut down to the bone. Carefully open and peek inside. The flesh should be white and tender; keep in mind that the fish will continue to cook after it leaves the oven, so don't overcook it.

Remove the fish to a warm serving platter, cover it lightly with foil, and set aside in a warm place.

Move the roasting pan to the stovetop over high heat. Add a drizzle of oil, if needed, then add the remaining garlic. When the garlic just begins to brown, add the tomatoes, chili, bay leaves, olives, and lemon zest.

Stir the vegetables and cook until they are heated through, then add the onions and artichokes; stir carefully to keep the artichokes from breaking apart. When everything is hot, add the basil and chives and quickly pour the ragout over the fish. The ragout should take 6 to 8 minutes altogether.

Garnish the platter with fresh herbs and warm Garlic Confit. Drizzle a little of the oil from the confit over the fish and squeeze fresh lemon juice over everything just before serving. Sprinkle a few grains of coarse sea salt on top.

HINT: Timing is the most important aspect of executing this dish. Cooking whole fish is actually easy, if you have the correct roasting pan and a hot oven. During the summer, grill fish outside. The ragout can be made ahead of time and reheated on the side of the fire.

POACHED PURPLE AND YELLOW PLUMS WITH LAVENDER SORBET

2 cups white wine such as Chardonnay

⅔ cup lavender honey (or regular honey)

½ cup sugar

1 bunch fresh lavender, or ¼ cup dried, untreated lavender flowers (see Note)

5 strips lemon zest made with a vegetable peeler

Juice of 2 lemons

5 strips of lime zest made with a vegetable peeler

Juice of 2 limes

2 sticks cinnamon

2 tablespoons chopped fresh ginger

Pinch salt

8 yellow plums, washed, halved, stems removed

5 black or purple plums, washed, stems removed, cut into thin wedges

6 candied lavender sprigs (see Hint), or mint leaves

In summer, the rolling hills in the south of France are covered by endless zebra stripes of lavender in many shades of purple. Make sure the lavender you use, dried or fresh, is untreated. Fresh flowers can be found in farmers' markets, and dried ones can be ordered through the mail—or dry your own crop to use all winter long. (Pictured on page 2.)

Place all ingredients except the plums in a large saucepan and bring to a boil; reduce the heat and simmer for 5 minutes. Remove the pan from the heat and steep the ingredients for 30 minutes. Place the plums in a large bowl. Warm the syrup slightly, pour it over the fruit, and refrigerate up to 4 days.

When the fruit and syrup are cold, strain off the syrup, reserving about 1 cup to use as a sauce, and pour the rest of the syrup into an ice-cream maker. Freeze according to the manufacturer's instructions.

To serve, place several plums of each color in a glass dish with some poaching syrup. Top with a scoop of sorbet and garnish with candied lavender.

NOTE: Lavender flowers are available from spice merchants (see Mail Order Sources, page 171).

HINTS: To make candied lavender, dip 2-inch flower tops in lightly whipped egg whites, then roll them in granulated sugar. Place on a nonstick baking sheet in a very low oven to dry. The lavender sprigs are good for stirring hot tea or for decorating cakes and tarts.

Peaches are a nice way to vary this dessert. They will produce a lighter-colored sorbet.

If your fruit is underripe, you may need to cook it slightly in the syrup until it just begins to become tender. Take care not to overcook it or it will become a purée. When the fruit is tender, remove it with a slotted spoon and place in the refrigerator to chill.

REAL FOOD BASICS

SECRET INGREDIENTS

These chutneys, vinegars, oils, and sauces will add new dimensions to your cooking. They offer hundreds of creative possibilities as you discover new uses for them, and they can help make the most of your garden or farmers' market.

Many of the recipes are modern adaptations of traditional German, English, and American methods. My family has used some of them for years, preserving the herbs, vegetables, and fruits from our Hoosier garden. Others have European, North African, Middle Eastern, and Asian influences.

OILS

CURRY OIL

Use this oil as a flavorful swirl around almost anything. Add vinegar or lemon juice and it becomes a curry vinaigrette for pasta and grain salads.

- 3 tablespoons curry powder
- 1 shallot, minced
- 2 cloves garlic, minced
- 1 teaspoon honey
- 2 cups canola oil

MAKES 2 CUPS

Combine the curry powder, shallot, garlic, honey, and 1 tablespoon water in a heavy-bottomed saucepan. Cook slowly over low heat until most of the liquid evaporates. Add the oil and stir well. Allow the mixture to cool to room temperature, then pour it into a clean, dry jar and store, covered, in the refrigerator for up to 2 months.

HINTS: I like to leave the solids in the oil, but you may strain them out by pouring the oil through several layers of cheesecloth.

Paprika, turmeric, dried ginger, wasabi, cinnamon, and cumin also can be used.

TRUFFLE AND OLIVE OIL PURÉE

Use this as a special treat when you are feeling the world is a terrible place to let you know that everything is all right. This is great tossed with pasta, spread on crostini, in salad dressing, or to dress poached fish.

- 2 to 3 fresh truffles, washed
- ½ cup olive oil
- ¼ teaspoon chopped garlic
- Sea salt
- Freshly ground pepper

MAKES ¾ CUP

Grind the truffles in a food processor with ¼ cup of the olive oil and the garlic to make a fine purée. With a rubber spatula scrape the purée into a small saucepan and warm it over medium heat; season to taste with salt and pepper. Remove the pan from the heat, add the remaining oil, and allow the mixture to cool to room temperature. Store the purée in the freezer and use a little at a time as needed; it will keep for about 4 months.

HINT: This is great finished with a little lemon zest brunoise and lemon juice.

ANCHOVY AND CHILI OIL

This is fabulous with sliced tomato and onion salad as well as on grilled vegetables and steamed cauliflower and broccoli. Try drizzling it on pasta, focaccia, pizza, and in Caesar dressing.

- 5 anchovy fillets
- 1 fresh cayenne or Thai chili pepper
- ¼ teaspoon garlic powder
- 2 cups extra-virgin olive oil

MAKES 2 CUPS

Dice 2 anchovies and place them in a clean, dry bottle. Add the remaining anchovies, the chili, garlic, and oil. Put the lid on the bottle and store in a cool, dark place for 1 week, shaking it daily. Shake before using. The oil keeps for up to 2 months in a cool, dark place.

VINEGARS

SPICED GARLIC VINEGAR

This is great in vinaigrettes and chilled mayonnaise or in Regime Sour Cream-based sauces. I also like it sprinkled over grilled meats and vegetables and in cold pasta and vegetable salads.

- 12 to 15 cloves garlic, peeled
- 1 bay leaf
- 10 peppercorns
- 1 dried cayenne pepper
- 4 cups good-quality red or white wine vinegar

MAKES 4 CUPS

Place the garlic and spices in a jar and cover them with the vinegar. Close the container with a cork or tight lid, and let it sit in a cool, dark place for at least 1 week. Add more vinegar as it is used up. Store the vinegar in a cool, dark place for up to 4 months.

ROSEMARY CABERNET VINEGAR

Use Cabernet wine vinegar if you can find it; it has a wonderful complexity.

  1 cup fresh rosemary branches, washed and dried with a towel

  3 cups Cabernet or other red wine vinegar

  2 cloves garlic

  10 peppercorns

MAKES 3 CUPS

Combine the ingredients in a jar and close it with a cork or tight lid. Allow it to sit in a cool, dark place for 1 month. Strain the vinegar through a coffee filter into a bottle and garnish it with a fresh rosemary sprig. Store the vinegar in a cool, dark place for up to 6 months.

THAI GINGER RICE VINEGAR

This is great in Asian-inspired salads and sprinkled over rice dishes.

  3 to 4 inches fresh ginger, peeled and finely chopped

  2 to 3 cloves garlic, peeled

  1 tablespoon honey

  3 cups rice vinegar

MAKES 3 CUPS

Combine the ingredients in a jar and close it with a cork or tight lid. Allow it to sit in a cool, dark place for 1½ to 2 weeks. Strain the vinegar into a bottle through cheesecloth or a coffee filter. Store the vinegar for up to 1 month at room temperature.

VINAIGRETTES

■

DANIEL'S BASIC VINAIGRETTE

  3 tablespoons good-quality Spanish sherry vinegar such as Xeres

  Juice of 1 lemon

  ½ teaspoon dry mustard

  ½ teaspoon Master Blend (page 167)

  1 clove garlic, minced

  1 small shallot, minced

  ½ teaspoon salt

  10 turns of a pepper mill

  ¾ cup virgin olive oil

MAKES APPROXIMATELY 1 CUP

Combine all the ingredients except the olive oil in a stainless steel bowl and whisk well. Continuing to whisk, gradually incorporate the oil. Taste and adjust the seasoning with salt, pepper, and lemon juice as needed. Store, covered, in the refrigerator for up to 2 weeks.

HINT: Variations can be made by replacing some of the olive oil with walnut or hazelnut oil and replacing the sherry vinegar with champagne vinegar or herb-flavored vinegar.

DANIEL'S CAESAR DRESSING

This is enough for two large Caesar salads. It also makes a great dip.

  1 coddled egg yolk (from a 2-minute boiled egg)

  1 clove garlic, minced

  ¼ teaspoon grated lemon zest

  1 teaspoon good-quality Spanish sherry vinegar such as Xeres

  Juice of 1 lemon

  ½ teaspoon mustard powder

  ¼ teaspoon Master Blend (page 167)

  5 drops hot pepper sauce such as Tabasco

  3 anchovy fillets, finely chopped

  2 tablespoons freshly grated Parmigiano-Reggiano

  1 teaspoon Worcestershire sauce

  ⅓ cup olive oil

  Salt

  Freshly ground pepper

MAKES ⅔ CUP

Combine all the ingredients except the oil, salt, and pepper in a stainless steel bowl and whisk well. Continuing to whisk, gradually incorporate the oil. Season to taste with salt and pepper. The extra can be stored, covered, in the refrigerator for up to 3 days.

TOMATO VINAIGRETTE

Use this more as a sauce than a dressing, either warm or at room temperature. Spoon a little around warm goat cheese or a vegetable terrine for a beautiful presentation.

  2 tablespoons extra-virgin olive oil

  1 clove garlic, minced

  1 cup chopped tomatoes (choose the ripest Roma, cherry, or Marmande)

  Pinch salt

  Pinch superfine sugar

  Dash sherry vinegar

  Freshly ground pepper

MAKES 1 CUP

Heat the oil in a small, nonreactive saucepan; add the garlic to lightly toast. Quickly add the tomatoes, salt, sugar, vinegar, and pepper. Bring to a boil, then purée with a hand mixer or in a blender. Pass the mixture through a fine sieve and adjust the seasoning to taste. Let cool to room temperature, then store, covered, in the refrigerator for up to 1 week.

POPPYSEED VINAIGRETTE

  3 tablespoons lemon juice

  4 tablespoons olive oil

  1 teaspoon honey

  ¼ teaspoon Master Blend (page 167)

  1 tablespoon poppyseeds

  Salt

  Freshly ground pepper

Combine all the ingredients, seasoning to taste with salt and pepper; set aside.

WASABI VINAIGRETTE

Use this with seaweed salad, seafood salad, chicken salad, or a salad of bitter greens, cucumbers, and radishes.

1 teaspoon wasabi powder

¼ teaspoon yellow mustard powder

2 tablespoons white vinegar

1 small clove garlic, finely chopped

1 teaspoon grated fresh ginger

1 coddled egg yolk (from a 2-minute boiled egg)

¼ cup safflower oil

Juice of ½ lemon

Salt

Freshly ground pepper

MAKES ½ CUP

In a medium-sized stainless steel bowl combine the wasabi and mustard powder, vinegar, garlic, ginger, and egg yolk; whisk well. Continuing to whisk, gradually incorporate the oil. Season to taste with the lemon juice and salt and pepper. Store, covered, in the refrigerator for up to 5 days

LEMON, SOY, AND GINGER VINAIGRETTE

Use this on chilled seafood salads or grilled vegetables.

½ cup mushroom soy sauce (see Note)

½ cup lemon juice

1 tablespoon grated fresh ginger

1 clove garlic, minced

¼ teaspoon crushed red pepper

2 cups olive oil

Salt

Freshly ground pepper

MAKES 3 CUPS

Combine the ingredients in a blender or food processor; blend for 30 to 40 seconds and adjust the seasoning with salt and pepper. To make the vinaigrette less likely to separate, add several tablespoons of boiling water and blend for 10 to 15 seconds more. Store, covered, in the refrigerator for up to 2 weeks.

NOTE: Mushroom soy sauce is available in Asian markets and health food stores.

SAUCES

■

DANIEL'S HOMEMADE MUSTARD

2 tablespoons mustard powder

3 tablespoons yellow mustard seeds

1 tablespoon wasabi powder

1 teaspoon ground turmeric

1 teaspoon Master Blend (page 167)

¼ teaspoon cinnamon

¼ cup white wine vinegar

¼ cup dry white wine

2 tablespoons honey

2 tablespoons olive oil

1 clove garlic, finely chopped

1 teaspoon salt

MAKES ½ CUP

In a small, heavy-bottomed, nonreactive saucepan combine all the spices except the salt with ⅔ cup water and bring to a boil. Reduce the heat and simmer for 8 minutes, stirring often. Remove the pan from the heat and allow the mixture to sit for 8 hours or overnight for the flavor to develop.

Add the vinegar, wine, honey, oil, garlic, and salt and bring to a boil. Reduce the heat and simmer for 5 to 10 minutes. Purée the mixture in a blender and adjust the seasoning with additional vinegar or mustard and salt as needed. Let the mustard cool to room temperature, then store, covered, in the refrigerator for up to 3 months.

MUSTARD HERB SAUCE

¼ cup mayonnaise, homemade or commercial

2 tablespoons green herb mustard

1 tablespoon parsley juice (see Note, page 99)

1 tablespoon chopped parsley

3 tablespoons chopped tarragon

3 tablespoons chopped chives

1 teaspoon minced lemon zest

5 drops hot pepper sauce such as Tabasco

Salt to taste

Freshly ground pepper

MAKES ½ CUP

Combine the ingredients well, taste, and adjust the seasoning as necessary.

SPICY PINK SAUCE

¼ cup mayonnaise, homemade or commercial

Juice of ½ lemon

2 tablespoons chopped capers

4 tablespoons chili sauce

15 drops hot pepper sauce such as Tabasco

1 teaspoon chopped parsley

MAKES ⅓ CUP

Combine the ingredients well, taste, and adjust the seasoning as necessary.

SPICY GARLIC PASTE

This is great on everything savory—from sandwiches and cold leftovers, to pastas, pizzas, and grilled meats, and in sauces, vinaigrettes, and stuffings.

10 heads garlic, separated into cloves

½ cup plus about 1 tablespoon olive oil

1 tablespoon fresh rosemary leaves

1 teaspoon sea salt

½ teaspoon freshly cracked black pepper

1 teaspoon Chinese garlic and chili paste

MAKES 2 CUPS

Preheat the oven to 350° F.

Peel the garlic cloves and place them on a double thickness of aluminum foil on a small baking sheet with ½ cup oil, the rosemary, sea salt, and pepper. Fold the sides in and seal the foil by crimping the edges. Bake the garlic for about 1 hour, until the garlic is very tender. Remove it from the oven, open the packet, and allow the garlic to cool to room temperature. Place the garlic and any oil in the bowl of a food processor and purée it with the chili paste. Adjust the seasoning with salt and pepper. Transfer the paste to a small jar and top with a thin layer of oil. Store, covered, in the refrigerator for up to 1 month.

NOTE: Chinese garlic and chili paste can be found in most Asian markets and in the Asian food sections of some supermarkets.

THAI HOT SAUCE

Serve this sauce with noodle dishes as well as with grilled meats and fish.

2 tablespoons tiny dried shrimp (see Note)

4 cloves garlic, peeled and roughly chopped

2 dried Thai chili peppers

1 teaspoon chopped fresh ginger

2 teaspoons honey

3 tablespoons Asian fish sauce

Juice of 2 limes

2 fresh green serrano chilies, seeded and finely diced

1 scallion, very thinly sliced

MAKES ⅓ CUP

In a blender, combine the shrimp, garlic, dried chilies, ginger, honey, fish sauce, and lime juice. Purée the ingredients to a paste, scraping the sides to make sure everything is thoroughly incorporated. Transfer the mixture to a small mixing bowl and stir in the fresh chilies and scallion. Store in the refrigerator for up to 2 weeks. The sauce is better after 24 hours.

NOTE: Dried shrimp and fish sauce can be found in Asian markets.

MOROCCAN PEPPER SAUCE WITH ORANGE ZEST

This sauce is perfect for grilled foods such as skewered shrimp, swordfish steaks, and chicken breast; or rub it on a leg of lamb before roasting. It's great on sandwiches and in vegetable and chicken soups.

2 cloves garlic, roughly chopped

1 teaspoon orange zest brunoise (page 102)

1 teaspoon minced fresh ginger

1 small fresh chili pepper

1 tablespoon Master Blend (page 167)

1 teaspoon cumin seeds

1½ teaspoons paprika

1 teaspoon salt

¼ to ½ teaspoon crushed red pepper

2 tablespoons red wine vinegar

¼ cup olive oil

¼ cup chopped fresh cilantro

MAKES 1 CUP

Process all the ingredients except the cilantro together with 1 tablespoon water in a food processor or blender until the purée is smooth. Pour the purée into a small saucepan, bring to a boil over medium heat, and cook for 2 to 3 minutes; pour it over the cilantro and mix well. Serve hot or let the sauce cool to room temperature and store, covered, in the refrigerator for up to 2 weeks.

BRAZILIAN MÔLHO DE PIMENTA E LIMAO

This hot pepper and lemon sauce is served with Brazil's national dish, *feijoada*, in which pork and beans do the samba. Make this just before using so it retains its crunchy texture. It is a wonderfully fiery accompaniment to grilled meats and rice dishes.

1 teaspoon lemon zest brunoise (page 102)

½ cup lemon juice

1 medium Spanish onion, finely minced

2 cloves garlic, minced

5 pickled cayenne or Tabasco peppers, finely chopped, plus ¼ teaspoon of the pickling liquid

¼ cup finely chopped Italian parsley

¼ teaspoon Master Blend (page 167)

¼ teaspoon salt

MAKES 1 CUP

Combine the ingredients in a mixing bowl and allow them to sit at room temperature for at least 15 minutes before serving. Do not make this more than 1 hour in advance.

LEMON AND GINGER MISO SAUCE

This is perfect for tofu topped with a sprinkle of toasted walnuts and on grilled and chilled vegetables such as turnips, carrots, and parsnips.

½ cup white miso (see Note)

½ tablespoon honey

3 tablespoons mirin (rice wine)

1 egg yolk

2 tablespoons finely chopped walnuts

½ teaspoon commercial ginger paste (see Note)

½ teaspoon lemon zest brunoise (page 102)

Salt

Freshly ground pepper

MAKES ¾ CUP

Combine the ingredients in a blender, seasoning to taste with salt and pepper, and purée until smooth. Pour the mixture into a small, heavy-bottomed, stainless steel saucepan and cook over low heat, stirring, until the sauce is slightly thick and shiny, 8 to 10 minutes; do

not let the sauce boil. Pour the sauce into a serving bowl and adjust the seasoning. Serve warm over steamed tofu or vegetables. Store the extra, covered, in the refrigerator for up to 5 days.

NOTE: White miso and ginger paste are available in Asian markets.

SPICY PONZU SAUCE (JAPANESE LEMON SOY SAUCE)

This is a typical dipping sauce that I like to serve with raw oysters and clams. It is also good for fish, chicken, and prawns.

¼ cup lemon juice

¼ cup mushroom soy sauce

1 tablespoon tamari

¼ teaspoon Chinese chili paste with garlic

¼ teaspoon lemon zest brunoise (page 102)

¼ teaspoon garlic paste

Hot pepper sauce such as Tabasco

MAKES ½ CUP

Combine all the ingredients in a nonreactive bowl, seasoning to taste with hot pepper sauce, and mix well. Store at room temperature for 2 to 3 days or refrigerated for 1 week.

NOTE: Use Meyer lemons if you can find them; they are closer in flavor to Japanese yuzu.

RED WINE SAUCE

Use this sauce with grilled or roasted meats, poultry, and fish.

2 tablespoons unsalted butter

½ pound shallots, peeled and thinly sliced

1 tablespoon tomato paste

1 bay leaf

1 sprig fresh thyme

2 teaspoons lightly crushed peppercorns

1 cup port

2 quarts deep red wine such as Burgundy or Rioja

2 quarts Veal Stock (page 166)

MAKES 1 QUART

In a large stock pot over high heat melt the butter and allow it to lightly brown. Add the shallots and reduce the heat to medium. Add the tomato paste, bay leaf, thyme, and pepper-

1 stalk celery

1 large section fennel bulb, roughly chopped

4 lemon slices

1 piece lemongrass, thinly sliced

2 branches fresh thyme

2 bay leaves, fresh if possible

15 peppercorns, crushed

3 allspice berries

1 teaspoon Master Blend (page 167)

2 teaspoons sea salt

2 cups white wine

Combine all the ingredients with 1 quart water in a large pot and bring to a boil; reduce the heat and simmer for 20 to 25 minutes. Strain the stock through a chinoise or a strainer lined with rinsed cheesecloth, using a ladle to press out the liquid. Season to taste.

Cool the stock to room temperature, then refrigerate or freeze until needed.

CHICKEN STOCK

5 pounds chicken bones (backs, wings, and necks)

3 medium onions, peeled and roughly chopped

1 medium celery root, peeled and chopped

1 medium carrot, peeled and chopped

1 head garlic, cut in half crosswise

1 parsnip, peeled and roughly chopped

½ pound leeks, white part only, chopped and washed

½ pound white mushrooms, chopped

2 fresh bay leaves

5 fresh sprigs thyme

½ bunch Italian parsley leaves and stems

1 teaspoon white peppercorns, crushed

2 cloves

1 teaspoon salt

MAKES 3 QUARTS, 1 CUP

Trim all the fat from the bones and wash them in cold water to remove any blood.

Place the bones in a 3-gallon or larger stock pot and cover with cold water.

Bring to a low boil and skim thoroughly; reduce the heat to a simmer. Add the remaining ingredients and simmer for 2 hours, skimming and tasting often.

Strain the stock and cool it quickly in an ice bath.

HINT: Add a whole chicken to the pot during the last hour of cooking. The stock will have a pleasant, fresh, meaty flavor, and you will have a poached chicken for dinner or to chill for a salad.

VEGETABLE STOCK

1 large onion, roughly chopped

2 to 3 leeks, white part only, roughly chopped and washed

4 shallots, chopped

1 cup chopped celery root

1 cup chopped carrots

1 parsnip, peeled and roughly chopped

4 tomatoes, seeded and chopped

3 cloves garlic, cut in half

2 stalks lemongrass, cut in half lengthwise and roughly chopped

½ bunch Italian parsley leaves and stems

2 fresh bay leaves

5 sprigs fresh thyme

8 white peppercorns, crushed

1 tablespoon fennel seeds

1 tablespoon coriander seeds

2 tablespoons sea salt

2 pieces star anise

MAKES 1 GALLON

Place the vegetables in a large stock pot, cover with cold water, and bring to a low boil.

Add the herbs and spices and simmer slowly for 1 hour, skimming and tasting often.

Strain the stock and cool it quickly in an ice bath.

HINTS: To make brown vegetable stock, preheat the oven to 450° F. Place the onions, leeks, shallots, celery root, carrots, and parsnips in a roasting pan with 2 tablespoons olive oil and roast them in the oven until brown; add 1 tablespoon tomato paste and continue to brown for 5 minutes longer. Transfer to a large stock pot on the stove top and add water to cover and the remaining ingredients; continue as for vegetable stock.

The vegetables and herbs all should be in peak condition; damaged or wilted vegetables have lost most of their nutritional value and flavor.

VEAL STOCK

5 pounds veal bones, shin and neck if possible

1 cup fresh crushed tomatoes, or ½ cup tomato paste

1(750-ml) bottle dark red wine such as Burgundy

3 medium onions, peeled and chopped

1 medium celery root, peeled and chopped

3 medium carrots, peeled and chopped

1 head garlic, cut in half crosswise

2 medium leeks, white part only, chopped and washed

2 cloves

1 teaspoon peppercorns, crushed

1 fresh bay leaf

5 sprigs fresh thyme

½ bunch parsley leaves and stems

MAKES 1 GALLON

Place a roasting pan in the oven and preheat the oven to 400° F.

Place the bones in the pan and brown for about 30 minutes, turning often. When the bones begin to color, spread the tomatoes over and continue to brown them. If the pan begins to over-color, add a cup or two of cold water.

Remove the bones from the pan and place them in a stock pot. Drain the fat from the pan and reserve. Place the pan over medium-high heat and deglaze the pan with the wine, stirring with a wooden spoon to scrape and incorporate the browned bits stuck to the pan. Cook to reduce the liquid by half; add the reduced liquid to the stock pot.

Cover the bones with cold water and bring to a low boil; skim completely, then reduce the heat and simmer gently, skimming often, for 2 hours; do not allow the liquid to come to a boil.

In a skillet heat the reserved fat and sauté the vegetables until they are browned.

Add the vegetables, spices, and herbs to the stock.

Simmer for 3 hours longer, tasting occasionally and skimming often; be sure the bones are covered with liquid during cooking and top with cold water as needed.

Strain the stock and cool it quickly in an ice bath.

SPICE BLENDS

∎

These spice blends are designed to bring an enormous range of flavor to dishes while cutting back on fats. You will find hundreds of ways to use them, whether preparing a Regime Cuisine dish or a Menu for Entertaining.

Make small batches of the mixes so they stay fresh, and don't worry if you are unable to come up with every ingredient—feel free to substitute or adjust quantities. Keep your blends handy so you won't forget about them. Put them in decorative containers that will keep them fresh while bringing visual intrigue to your kitchen. (Pictured on page 7.)

MASTER BLEND

This is great on everything. Add the blend to bacon during the last third of cooking; sautéed chicken livers, scallops, shrimp; roasts of all kinds; stuffing; pâtés and terrines; Persian rice; and slow-cooked green beans with tomatoes. Use it as a rub for poultry before roasting and in dredging flour for sautés.

> 3 tablespoons coriander
> 2 pieces star anise
> 1 tablespoon fennel seeds, half raw, half toasted
> 2 teaspoons mustard seeds
> 5 cardamom seeds
> 1 teaspoon cumin seeds
> 1 teaspoon ginger powder
> 1 (½-inch) stick cinnamon
> 1 teaspoon white peppercorns
> 1 teaspoon black peppercorns
> 3 dried bay leaves
> ½ teaspoon whole mace

Grind together finely in a spice grinder.

MIXED PEPPER BLEND (AUX POIVRES)

Use to season roasted jumbo sea scallops; venison chops with juniper; seared spiced tuna fillet; and as a crust for New York sirloin steaks. Sprinkle on soups and salads for a peppery crunch.

Mix with Master Blend (above) and brown sugar for "oven barbecued" salmon fillets, or with Mellow Yellow (below) to rub on pork roast.

> 2 tablespoons cracked white pepper
> 2 tablespoons cracked black pepper
> 1 teaspoon crushed red pepper (cayenne)
> 3 tablespoons crushed fennel seeds
> 4 tablespoons crushed coriander seeds
> 2 tablespoons crushed Szechuan pepper
> 1 teaspoon crushed Guinea pepper

Blend the ingredients together thoroughly.

MELLOW YELLOW

Use to spice goat cheese; lamb and chicken dishes; carrots with mint in spiced vinaigrette; chickpea salad; basmati rice; monkfish with apples; cauliflower with capers, olives, and tomatoes; eggplant purée; potato purée with roasted garlic; Cuban roast chicken with yellow rice; and Moroccan tomato confit with honey.

> 1 teaspoon mustard seeds
> 1 teaspoon cardamon seeds
> ½ teaspoon fennel seeds
> 1 teaspoon ginger powder
> ¼ teaspoon saffron
> 2 teaspoons ground turmeric
> 1 teaspoon coriander seeds
> 1 teaspoon white peppercorns
> 1 teaspoon dried orange zest

Grind together finely in a spice grinder.

SWEET SPICES

Use in oatmeal with raisins; caramelized carrots with pearl onions; pies and pastries; baked apples; vanilla custard or crème brûlée; broiled mackerel with lemon; shrimp and scallop stew with ginger; and Moroccan couscous.

Make fruit spreads by simmering dried apples, pears, or apricots with water, honey, and Sweet Spices until tender; chill and use to replace butter on the breakfast table.

> 1 teaspoon ginger powder
> 1 (½-inch) stick cinnamon
> ½ teaspoon annatto seeds
> ½ teaspoon pomegranate powder
> 2 teaspoons fennel seeds
> 2 pieces star anise
> 2 cardamom seeds
> 2 teaspoons coriander seeds
> 3 cloves
> 1 piece mace
> ¼ teaspoon ground nutmeg
> 2 dried bay leaves

Grind finely in a spice grinder.

RUSSIAN RED SPICES

Use in beet salad; stuffed cabbage; braised red cabbage; borscht; venison escallops with sautéed apples and spices; chicken thighs with sweet potatoes, lemon, and dried apricots; game dishes; and tomato chowder with spiced croutons.

> 1 (½-inch) stick cinnamon
> ½ teaspoon caraway seeds
> 1 teaspoon annatto seeds
> 1 teaspoon ginger powder
> 1 teaspoon fennel seeds
> 1 piece star anise
> 1 teaspoon Hungarian paprika
> ¼ teaspoon dried cayenne pepper
> 3 juniper berries
> ½ teaspoon dried orange peel

Grind finely in a spice grinder.

For information about where you can find Daniel Orr's spice blends and video call 800 824 2398 or e-mail tmatt@futuris.net.

DANIEL'S NOTEBOOK

■

ON SALT

I don't eliminate salt in my recipes, but I don't overuse it either. In most, salt is a "to taste" ingredient that you determine and control. I suggest specific amounts only when they will affect the outcome or success of a dish.

The salt I use every day is hand-raked sea salt from Brittany, France. The large crystals are slightly gray in color and taste wonderfully of the sea. These crystals not only enhance the flavors of the food, but they add a slight crunch or texture when added near the end of cooking or on a finished dish. These little salt "fixes," I believe, allow us to use less. A few grains of coarse sea salt sprinkled over a sliced piece of grilled meat will do more for its flavor than double the amount if used before cooking.

Seasoning with salt should be done at the end of cooking sauces and soups because in both, the liquids are reduced, which concentrates the salt and alters its proportion. The only exception is when a meat or vegetable is cooked in the sauce, as in stews or other braised dishes. In those, the morsels need time to absorb the other flavors, and salt should be added earlier.

I use salt in desserts, where it is often omitted. Small amounts of salt and pepper are included in recipes for ice creams, sorbets, syrups, and other desserts to balance the sweetness and allow you to use smaller amounts of butter and cream. A little salt, along with the juices and zests of citrus fruits, helps to keep sugar and fat to a minimum.

For the recipes in *Real Food*, gray sea salt or kosher salt should be used rather than iodized salt, which is highly refined and often contains colorless, odorless, and tasteless chemicals. Keep in mind that because of the size of the crystals kosher salt weighs 20 to 50 percent less than equal amounts of table salt.

ON POACHING

To some, poaching means bland—dry and stringy white chicken breasts or flaky fish. But when done with a deft hand and a dose of creativity poaching can yield moist and texturally pleasing, flavorful, and satisfying dishes.

The keys to success are well-flavored broths made with stocks, vegetables, herbs, spices, and wines or juices; slow and reverent cooking; and carefully observed timing. Problems occur with too high heat, cooking too long, and soul-less broths.

Besides beautifully turned-out dishes, poachers are rewarded with leftover broths that make wonderful bases for future soups and sauces, or richer poaching liquids for next time.

To save your poaching liquid, skim off the fat and strain the liquid well; if any fat remains, run a cold lettuce leaf across the surface to gather stray particles. Try poaching in broths made with smoked pheasant carcasses or other bones or scraps of smoked meats. The delicate flavors come through wonderfully. Teas, ginger, lemongrass, lime leaves, soy sauce, fish sauce, citrus peel, and just about anything else you can think of are worth a try.

METHOD

Bring your poaching liquid to a "shimmer"—the temperature between a simmer and a boil where the liquid moves slightly on the surface, but without bubbles.

Have whatever food you are poaching at room temperature (the shock from the rapid temperature change toughens the flesh) and carefully lower it into the liquid.

Bring the liquid back to a shimmer, and poach just until the food is cooked through, which will depend on the recipe. If you are poaching something to be served the following day, allow it to cool in its own broth. If you are serving soon after cooking, remove the item to a plate and cover it with a moist towel or plastic wrap; poached foods tend to dry out if left uncovered.

ON STEAMING

As in poaching, flavor is transferred from liquid by steaming, but while poaching gently bathes, steaming shocks with temperatures higher than those of boiling water.

Steaming is perfect for quick-cooking vegetables, meats, and starches. It also is a satisfactory method for more delicate items that can be wrapped in lettuce, cabbage, or even corn husks or starches like rice, wheat, or potato to protect and absorb the flavors of their contents.

I use steaming to reheat problematic leftovers to retain their moisture. Lightly steamed sushi that spent the night in the ice box comes back surprisingly fresh. I also reheat tamales, brown rice, couscous, and vegetables in my steamer.

Steaming is sometimes thought of as healthful but boring. However, when applied to the freshest of ingredients, steaming can be perfectly wonderful in its simplicity. The rationale for steaming goes beyond the practical: one of my favorite dishes is a baby chicken breast wrapped with seared foie gras and a savoy cabbage leaf and steamed—the result is rich, clean, and altogether memorable.

METHODS

- Heat water to a strong boil and place the steamer above. Fill the steamer with the items to be steamed and cover. Cook as instructed in the recipe.
- Place the item on a plate and add a little stock, wine, or water. Season with salt and pepper and cover the plate tightly with plastic wrap. Place the plate in the microwave oven and cook with high power until done. Carefully remove the plate with a potholder.

A word of caution: steaming can be dangerous. Steam is very, very hot, and a steam burn can be serious, so turn your face away and keep your potholders nearby.

ON SAUTÉING

When sautéing, the motion of arm and pan causes the contents to go airborne and, with luck, land back where they took off. For me this is a thoroughly enjoyable activity. Even as a child I would toss dry beans in a pan in imitation of the chefs who were my family's friends.

A small amount of oil is needed when sautéing in traditional pans. But now with teflon coating sautéing can actually be done with a bit of liquid. This combines the techniques of sautéing and steaming. So whether using a little olive oil, stocks, or water, this is one of the most fat-free ways to prepare food.

The high heat used in sautéing with liquids and oil sets color quickly and caramelizes the natural sugars that are released in cooking. In the process, flavors intensify as the ingredients combine.

When using only a fat, the technique is shallow frying, which brings crunchiness to the exteriors of starches and proteins. It is what brings the desired crispness to dishes like sautéed potatoes or sweetbreads.

ROASTING AND BRAISING 101

Roasting and braising are kissing cousins—closely related but uniquely different. Like a sauna, roasting draws out excess moisture and brings color to the skin. Though perfect for starches such as potatoes, and many vegetables, for me roasting is really about meats.

Roasting requires special pans and special utensils, but once you are secure with the method, they will be well worth the investment, because they will be in constant use. Buy a heavy-duty roasting pan that will hold heat, with fairly high sides to prevent splattering. The pan should always be just large enough to hold what you'll be cooking; use too large a pan and the drippings will burn and you'll lose the great asset of pan sauce. A pan that is too small results in uneven cooking, a dirty oven, and smoky kitchen.

You also need a good roasting fork. I found an old heavy one with a worn wooden handle at the flea market that is so comfortable it is like an extension of my hand, which is how any hand-held cooking tool, including a knife, should feel. A roasting fork should be strong with narrow, slightly angled points to prevent food from easily slipping off. For professional chefs, the fork is also a thermometer. Stick it into the center of the roast, allowing it to stay there a couple of seconds, then feel it on the wrist or lip. If the fork comes out cold, the roast is "bleu" or still raw; body temperature means rare; warm means medium-rare, and hot is medium to medium-well. If the fork brings tears to your eyes and a blister to your skin, it is well-done. This test is best left to professionals.

Once you have the equipment and a preheated oven (500° F.) you are ready to roast. Season meat well with sea salt and pepper and try some of my spice blends (page 167).

When roasting a large piece of meat, preheat the roasting pan in the oven in order to sear the exteriors. Smaller items may be seared on the stove top, then finished in the oven.

Searing is the most important part of roasting, though not for the reason that it seals in juices. What searing does is caramelize the natural sugars in the meat, fish, or vegetable, giving them deeper, more intense flavor, and transforming their texture. To sear in the oven, turn the roast enough times to caramelize all sides—usually two times for fish and two to four times for meat. Always turn and close the oven door quickly to prevent heat escaping. Once the roast is evenly browned, the oven temperature can be reduced to 350° F. or 375° F. for most items until finished.

Most roasts should be cooked rare to medium-rare. Serve the end slices to those who want medium to well-done. If you overcook the whole roast, there's no turning back. If you undercook a little, you can always pop it back in the oven. You also will have better leftovers; there's not much you can do with a lot of well-done roast beef.

I often add chopped vegetables such as carrots, onions, celery, leeks, and garlic during the last third of cooking. This helps prevent burning of the meat juices and adds dimension to your pan sauce. A little wine, stock, or water also may be added.

Always remove a roast a little before it reaches desired doneness as it will continue to cook for several minutes after it is removed from the oven. Check for doneness in the thickest section of the roast, and remember that the rest will be more cooked. Allow the roast to rest for 5 to 25 minutes, depending on its size. If you slice a roast right out of the oven, it will lose most of its juices and, consequently, much of its flavor, moisture, texture, and rosy color. This resting time also gives you the chance to make your sauce.

To make a pan sauce, pour off the juices and skim off the fat; I also pat the pan with some paper towels to absorb any left behind. Over high heat, deglaze the pan with wine, water, or stock; allow the liquid to reduce while scraping up the browned bits from the bottom with a wooden spoon.

Finish the sauce by straining and seasoning it, or make a more complicated sauce by adding a demi-glaze or by thickening it with a roux or other starch-based mixture. Or finish with a compound butter such as the truffle butter in the poussin recipe (page 151).

Roasting vegetables brings out natural sweetness and deepens flavors. They gain a meatiness and a richness no other cooking method can match. For best results simply toss root vegetables in a little olive oil and throw them in the hot oven. Turn them a couple of times until they are tender and evenly colored, then remove them. Serve roasted vegetables with a squeeze of lemon and a few grains of sea salt and fresh pepper.

BRAISING

If roasting is like a sauna, then braising is the Jacuzzi. Braising is done at a leisurely pace, perfuming the house with an aroma of richness and comfort. Braised dishes are usually made with lesser-grade meats that need the added cooking time and moisture to tenderize them. Braised dishes reheat well, and are often even better the second day.

For most braised dishes, follow the same methods as for roasting through searing. Add chopped vegetables, herbs, spices, and enough liquid to cover the meat by one-third to two-thirds. Reduce the oven temperature, and cover with a lid or aluminum foil. When the meat is tender, remove it and finish the sauce.

ON GRILLING

The most important thing to learn is when the coals are ready. Whether briquettes or hard-wood charcoal, you must use plenty, burn them until they are a dusty white ash with a red-hot interior, and cook close enough to the coals that heat sears and caramelizes what's above them. This gets easier with experience.

Finer points include: using a heavy grid that will retain heat and preheating it to prevent sticking; judging the amount of fire needed to cook all the food on hand; and starting the fire early enough that the crowd doesn't get drunk and unruly before the food is ready.

If you must cheat, natural gas grills are easily lighted, ready quickly, and produce more reliable levels of heat than propane grills—and you don't have to worry about running out of gas. My parents have been known to shovel a path through the snow to get to their grill for a midwinter fix of summer.

After grilling don't waste the hot coals in your charcoal pit or fireplace. Wrap garlic bulbs in several thicknesses of foil with a drizzle of olive oil, sea salt, and freshly ground pepper and place them at fire's edge for several hours until they are sweet and tender. Toss the garlic with vegetables or pasta, spread it on bread, or smash it with a little vinegar and add it to salad dressings.

ON GRAINS, BEANS, AND LEGUMES

Perfectly cooked grains are tender, fluffy, and have a nutty flavor and texture. Poorly cooked ones are either hard or a gooey mess. These problems are caused by over- or undercooking or from using too much water. Most grains need a ratio of 2 parts grain to 3 parts water, though a little more water may be needed. It is better to add water as needed during cooking than to use too much.

Most grains can be rinsed, covered with water, brought to a boil, then simmered until tender. Bulgur, on the other hand, is best sautéed lightly in oil for several minutes then topped with boiling water at a ratio of 4 parts grain to 5 parts water, cooked for 20 to 25 minutes and then fluffed with a fork. Millet is best poured directly into boiling water with a little olive oil, partially covered, and cooked for 15 to 20 minutes. It should be cooked quickly, then spread out in a dish or it will continue to cook. Salt millet after cooking. Wheat berries and barley are the longest cooking of the grains I regularly use. Wheat berries should be cooked for 50 to 55

minutes in a ratio of 4 cups water to 1 cup wheat berries.

Cooking grains in large batches allows you to execute several recipes without having to wait for the grains to cook. It also eliminates having to clean up a lot of pans. If you cook one or two grains a week, make extra and chill or freeze it. Frozen cooked grains retain most of their wonderful texture, and if mixed with other ingredients after defrosting, you won't notice the difference.

When cooking grains for cold salads or side dishes, rinse them under cold water to stop the cooking, and to wash off excess starch. Allow the grains to drain thoroughly before you toss them in vinaigrette or sauce. Always reseason the dishes after they sit: the grains absorb the flavors and the salads may become a little bland.

Before cooking, black beans, red beans, white beans, and navy beans should be soaked overnight in cold water. To avoid fermentation, keep the beans refrigerated while soaking. After soaking, the beans should be drained and cooked in fresh water. Cooking times will vary with the type of bean; allow 1½ to 2 hours for most. Never add salt to beans while they are cooking, or it will make them tough.

Lentils do not need to be soaked and will cook in 30 to 45 minutes.

MAIL ORDER SOURCES

Akron Prime Meats
1425 Third Avenue
New York, NY 10028
Tel: 212 744 1551
     800 600 1010
Organically fed, prime-quality meats

Aux Delice de Bois
4 Leonard Street
New York, NY 10013
Tel: 212 334 1230
Fax: 212 334 1231
Seasonal wild mushrooms and produce from France

Baldor Enterprises
4900 Maspeth Avenue
Maspeth, NY 11378
Tel: 718 456 1300
Fax: 718 456 5400
Fine fruits and herbs and vegetables by the case

Balducci's
424 Avenue of the Americas
New York, NY 10011
Tel: 212 673 2600
French and Italian products; various dried beans such as rice beans, Christmas beans, and Swedish brown beans

Baldwin Fish Market
1584 First Avenue
New York, NY 10028
Tel: 212 288 9032
Good-quality fish and seafood

Caviar House
170 Lombard Street
San Francisco, CA 94111
Tel: 415 693 9496
Fax: 415 693 0685
Fine caviar

Casa Moneo
210 West 14th Street
New York, NY 10011
Tel: 212 929 1644
Mexican and Latin American products

Central Fish
527 Ninth Avenue
New York, NY 10018
Tel: 212 279 2317
An unbelievable variety of fresh, cheap, and fabulous fish

Citarella
2135 Broadway at 75th Street
New York, NY 10023
Tel: 212 874 0383
A fashion show of fish, expensive but worth it

Commodities Natural
165 First Avenue at 10th Street
New York, NY 10003
Tel: 212 260 2600
An excellent selection of beans, noodles, rice, and pasta

D'Artagnan
399-419 St. Paul's Ave.
Jersey City, NJ 07306
Tel: 800 327 8246
Fax: 201 792 6113
Foie gras, game, confits, and homemade sausages and pâtés

Dean & Deluca, Inc.
560 Broadway
New York, NY 10012
Tel: 212 221 7714
     800 221 7714
World-class ingredients, meats, fish, produce

Foods of India
Sinha Trading Company, Inc.
120 Lexington Avenue
New York, NY 10016
Tel: 212 683 4419
Indian curries, chutneys, relishes, and pickles

Gourmet Garage
453 Broome Street at Mercer
New York, NY 10013
Tel: 212 535 5880
Fine produce, flowers, baked goods, cheeses, olives, and prepared items

Grace's Marketplace
1237 Third Avenue
New York, NY 10021
Tel: 212 737 0600
Fine gourmet foods

Ideal Cheese
1205 Second Avenue
New York, NY 10021
Tel: 800 382 0109
     212 688 7579
40-year-old landmark of fine cheeses

Integral Yoga
Natural Foods
229 West 13th Street at 8th Avenue
New York, NY 10011
Tel: 212 243 2642
     800 343 1735
Hard-to-find natural and health food ingredients at reasonable prices

Kalustyan's
124 Lexington Avenue
New York, NY 10016
Tel: 212 685 3451
Fax: 212 683 8458
Middle Eastern spices, grains, and curry powders

Katagiri
224 East 59th Street
New York, NY 10022
Tel: 212 755 3566
A wonderful Japanese market that carries other Asian ingredients as well

Macy's Cellar
The Market Place
151 West 34th Street
New York, NY 10001
Tel: 212 695 4400
A wide variety of fine foods, cheeses, and caviar

Nature's Wild Rice Company
P.O. Box 1593
Bemidji, MN 56601
Tel: 800 222 5085
Fax: 218 751 5564
Dried grains, fruits, spices, pastas, and peppers

New Zealand Gourmet
371 North Oak Street
Inglewood, CA 90303
Tel: 310 677 7866
Fax: 310 677 6137
Fresh venison products

Paprikas Weiss Importer
1572 Second Avenue
New York, NY 10028
Tel: 212 288 6117
Spices, nuts, and condiments

Pisacane Midtown
940 First Avenue
New York, NY 10022
Tel: 212 752 7560
Some of New York's best fish with local delivery available

Salumeria Biellese
376 Eighth Avenue
New York, NY 10001
Tel: 212 736 7376
Italian and French sausages and other charcu-
terie

Soho Provisions
518 Broadway
New York, NY 10012
Tel: 212 334 4311
Exotica at discount prices

Special Foods
6533 South Sepulveda Boulevard
Los Angeles, CA 90045
Tel: 310 641 0443
Fax: 310 641 0530
Fresh fish, shellfish, and specialty items

United Poultry
736 North Broadway
Los Angeles, CA 90012
Tel: 213 617 8522
Squab, duck, free-range chicken, and some
seafood

Urbani Truffles USA
29-24 40th Avenue
Long Island City, NY 11101
Tel: 718 392 5050
Fax: 718 392 1704
White and black truffles, caviar, dried mush-
rooms, and truffle juice and oil

Valrhona Chocolat
1901 Avenue of the Stars
Suite 1774
Los Angeles, CA 90067
Tel: 310 277 0401
Fax: 310 277 4092
Fine French chocolates

The Vinegar Factory
431 East 91st Street
New York, NY 10128
Tel: 212 987 0885
Fine foods, fish, meats, and prepared items

Williams-Sonoma
Mail Order Department
P.O. Box 7456
San Francisco, CA 94120-7456
Tel: 415 652 9007
A large selection of gourmet foods, cookware, and
serving utensils

Whole Foods in Soho
117 Prince Street
New York, NY 10012
Tel: 212 982 1000
A well-informed staff selling a wide variety of
healthful foods

Zabar's
2245 Broadway
New York, NY 10024
Tel: 212 787 2000
Fine foods, including caviar, cheeses, foie gras;
cookware

INDEX